Everyday
Confident

365 ways to a better you

Everyday

Confident

365 ways to a better you

Jane Garton

Illustrated by Michelle Tilly

spruce

An Hachette UK Company
First published in Great Britain in 2011 by Spruce
a division of Octopus Publishing Group Ltd
Endeavour House, 189 Shaftesbury Avenue
London, WC2H 8JY
www.octopusbooks.co.uk
www.octopusbooksusa.com

Distributed in the USA and Canada for Octopus Books USA
c/o Hachette Book Group USA
237 Park Avenue
New York, NY 10017

Produced by **Bookworx**
Editorial Jo Godfrey Wood, **Design** Peggy Sadler

ISBN 13 978-1-84601-334-8
ISBN 10 1-84061-334-8

A CIP catalogue record for this book is available from the British Library.

Printed and bound in China

10 9 8 7 6 5 4 3 2 1

Contents

Introduction

Would you like to be able to walk into a room with complete self-assurance? Have the courage of your convictions, no matter what the situation? Bag the job or partner of your dreams? It's all down to confidence.

Confidence is crucial to every aspect of life and has an impact on everything you do: education, work, bringing up children and your relationships. But what is confidence? And why do some of us have oodles of it while others have little or none?

The word 'confidence' comes from the Latin *confido* meaning 'I trust' (in someone). That someone is you. Confidence is about getting in touch with your inner self; the part of you that has the power to succeed at whatever you set out to do. And the good news is it is not a trait you are born with, but something you can learn as you go through life.

Not that confidence happens overnight. According to the experts it takes just 21 days to change a thought pattern, but longer for it to become a habit. So get started now.

In *Everyday Confident* you will find 365 tips on how to up your confidence quotient, at home, at work and at play. You will learn to tap into inner strengths you never knew you had, such as courage, determination, enthusiasm and resilience. You will learn to say 'I can' instead of 'I can't' and 'I will' instead of 'I won't'.

Either start on day one and follow the tips through to the end of the year or dip in and out as the mood takes you. And don't forget to fill in the checklists every four weeks to see how far you've come.

Above all, remember, confidence is an attitude of mind. As you will see in the following pages, you can boost it by changing the way you look at the world. If you tell yourself that you can't do something, the chances are you will fail. But if you believe in yourself, nine times out of ten you will succeed. Here's to the new confident you!

How to use this book

If you've bought this book as part of your plan for the New Year, that's fine, but if you've picked this book up at some time during the middle of the year, don't worry. It will still work for you. You can start any time you feel like it during the year; you don't have to start it on New Year's Day. Just turn to Day 1 and work your way through the days in order. You will find that the months have either 30 or 31 days to reflect the real year, so you might want to match the month you're in with one that has the correct number of days on offer (the first month has 31 days).

At the end of every month you'll find a page for assessing how you're getting on. This is simply an opportunity to think about what you've read and whether any of the ideas are working for you. There's also a space here to write down your thoughts and think about how you're progressing. Run out of writing space? Turn to the final pages of the book and you'll find more pages to continue any important personal notes.

1

Start small

Start a new project today, but resist jumping in at the deep end because chances are you'll drown! Instead, take the easiest steps first.

For example, if you decide to study something new, read the easiest books on the subject first. If you embark on a teach-yourself French course learn a few everyday words before you start listening to the tape.

Overcoming mini-challenges first will give you the necessary confidence to face any tougher ones that could lie ahead.

Follow the lead of many successful people and use encouraging self-talk to celebrate when you have achieved a goal. Don't be timid. Talk out loud in an excited tone and heap yourself with praise. Use phrases such as 'I've done it, I've done it!' and 'I am so clever.'

Also remember to tell yourself when you are doing well and putting your best effort into something, reminding yourself of all the positive benefits that lie ahead if you keep going. At the same time, be aware that negative 'cant's' and 'don't think so's' could have the reverse effect.

> We cannot always control our thoughts, but we can control our words, and repetition impresses the subconscious, and we are then master of the situation.
>
> Florence Scovel Shinn

3

Think past and present

USE YOUR HANDS
Use emphatic hand gestures when you are speaking in public. You will appear more confident. Research shows that an audience absorbs at least 15 per cent more information if a speaker uses their hands while talking.

Use the past and present to help you shape your confident future. Think about the people who have influenced you most during the past year and any events that have had a noticeable effect on your thought patterns.

Then, focus on the present. Who do you spend most of your time with? What is happening in the here and now?

Reflecting on the past and understanding and being honest about your current situation can help you to see where you want to go in the future.

Here's how to be phone-confident, especially if, for example, you don't like negotiating on the phone or can't put off that dreaded call for a minute longer. Do it standing up. You will immediately feel at a psychological and physical advantage.

Also try smiling as you talk. It may seem unlikely, but when you smile you immediately sound more confident and assertive and the person at the other end will respond accordingly.

5 Face up to problems

Tackle outstanding problems at work as they arise. Confident people face up to problems head on and work out ways to deal with them rather than putting them off for another day.

If you don't think you can handle something on your own, seek help. Talk through your dilemma with friends or co-workers, or write it down, finishing off with a list of hopeful solutions. It can also help to note down the pros and cons of each solution before making your final decision on the best action to take.

Take a couple of hours and compile a list of short- and long-term goals for yourself. These must be unique to you. They may range from losing weight to sorting out your finances or taking the steps you need to put yourself in line for a new career.

Start with small steps. Take each one in turn and make a detailed action plan to help drive you toward your larger long-term goals. Pin your list up where you can see it. The fridge door or a spot above your desk are both ideal. Get going on your first target and watch your confidence grow as you accomplish each stage.

Remember, to be effective goals should be specific, measurable, achievable, realistic and time-based.

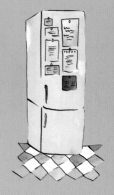

7

Adopt a role model

Spend half an hour thinking about which co-workers you have admired during the past six months. What is it about them that you find appealing? Do they have qualities that you admire? Perhaps it is their communication or people-management skills or perhaps it's simply the image they project.

Learning from role models can be a great way to develop confidence in the workplace, so think hard if there is anything you can learn from them to drive you forward.

Instant confidence

UP THE JEWELRY
Don't keep buying endless bits of cheap jewelry. Instead, save your money and go for one amazing statement piece. You'll find it will exude confidence on your behalf.

Be a bookworm

Visit your local library or bookstore and browse through the various sections. Your aim is to feed your brain with as much information as you think it can take. Be a bit selective, though, and scan shelves for books on subjects you are the most interested in. That way you are more likely to borrow or buy books that you will really enjoy reading.

Knowledge boosts self-confidence, and a good grasp of what's going on in the literary world will help you strike up conversations that really mean something. It will also ensure that you're not left out of group discussions at social occasions.

Confidence is the bond of friendship.

Publilius Syrus

9

Learn to say 'no'

The word 'no' is one of the most empowering words in any language, but also one of the hardest to say. The key is to speak it with quiet assertion rather than aggression. Learn to say 'no' to anything or anyone that is draining your confidence or is not serving your best interests.

If you find 'no' a difficult word to say, practice can bring perfection. Stand in front of a mirror and let your mouth form the word 'no'. Then think of someone you would like to be able to stand up to. Visualize yourself saying 'no' to them and then imagine how great you will feel afterward.

Habits change into character.

Ovid

Stick up for yourself

Search out a friend, relative or co-worker who always tends to put you down. Today you are going to start sticking up for yourself. Be firm and let them know, in no uncertain terms, that their opinion of you is not held by everyone and, most of all, not by you.

This may be hard the first time you do it, but once you get used to sticking up for yourself your confidence will grow and there will be no stopping you.

Instant confidence

PUT YOUR FEET UP

OK, we all know that putting your feet up is good for your circulation, but it can also induce feelings of calm and relaxation, making you feel instantly confident about yourself.

11 Create boundaries

Be a 'yes' person and you risk ending up stressed and overworked, not to mention low in self-esteem. So next time your boss tries to pile even more into your ever-growing in-tray consider whether you need, or have time, to take on extra work.

Think about what you really feel. If you think the extra work is going to make you angry, resentful and put upon, it's time to create a new boundary. Make up your mind as to how much you are prepared to take on and stick to your decision. You can still be a good employee while saying 'enough is enough'.

> If I have the belief that I can do it, I shall surely acquire the capacity to do it even if I may not have it at the beginning.
>
> Mahatma Gandhi

Dress to impress

Make sure you've got a good classic jacket in your wardrobe, ready to wear to meetings or interviews. You can get away with more ordinary trousers and skirts, as well as sweaters and shirts for wearing underneath, but spending money on a stylish, well-cut jacket is worth every penny, every time. So splash out on something special. It will take you places, giving you power, influence and confidence.

13

Write before you speak

If you've got an important speech or complaint to make it's very important to appear 100 percent self-assured. Achieve this by planning what you want to say and writing it down before the great event so that you can make maximum impact. All the great politicians and orators spend hours agonizing over their words. But don't read out your speech word for word. Write key points onto index cards to use as quick reminders and then speak from your heart.

Also, remember, fewer words are often more effective than disjointed ramblings, so your message is best kept simple and direct. That way it is easy on the ear and will hold the attention of your audience.

Of course, it is good to delegate, but in so doing you could be boosting someone else's morale at the expense of your own. This is how it goes: a problem or a task presents itself; your low self-esteem gets you thinking that you can't do it, so you rush off to enlist someone else to do it instead of you. The result? The other person wins all the glory and gets a huge boost to their self-esteem while you have deprived yourself of the confidence that the achievement might have brought you.

So next time a problem presents itself don't be so hasty to delegate it; at least give yourself the chance to have a go at dealing with it.

15

Get computer-confident

The more you see yourself as what you'd like to become, and act as if what you want is already there, the more you'll activate these dormant forces that will collaborate to transform your dream into your reality.

Dr Wayne W Dyer

The days are now long gone when you could get away with being computer illiterate. Somebody finding out that you can't make, or even understand, the simplest computer moves can send your confidence levels into freefall.

Explore the different software available and scour guides to help the nervous and the technophobic; there are plenty to choose from out there. If you still can't get to grips with technology, enrol in a class for beginners and sharpen up your keyboard skills as fast as you can. It will perk up your confidence no end.

Putting off what you can do today until tomorrow just makes you feel bad about yourself. Research also shows that 'putter-offers' are more likely to suffer from stress than those who get things done.

So say goodbye to procrastination and draw up a list of the things that you have been meaning to do but haven't yet set a date for, and stick to it. Think about the time and the energy you have wasted worrying about not getting things done, not to mention the guilt. It's simply not worth it, is it? If the list is very long you may not be able to do it all at once. But, there's no time like the present, so, even if you can't complete everything in one go, get started NOW.

Instant confidence

SKIPPITY SKIP
Buy yourself a jump rope and get outside. If you don't own a patio or green patch go to your nearest park and start moving.

Reassess your goals

Why not revisit your life goals from time to time, to keep you fresh and confident? Check your goals' sell-by dates. If you find they have served their purpose and life seems repetitive, then it's time to reassess them.

First take stock of any progress you have made and pat yourself on the back for whatever you've achieved so far. Then decide where you want to go next. Finally, make a list of your new goals, ensuring they are challenging, and you will instantly feel re-inspired and re-energized.

Are you a lark or an owl? Some of us feel more awake, and hence more confident, first thing in the morning, while others come to life when the sun goes down. Think carefully about when you feel at your most positive and arrange all your activities accordingly.

For example, if you usually feel flaky when you first get into work schedule important meetings and phone calls to happen later in the day. Similarly, you might feel more alert on a Monday rather than toward the end of the week. Be aware of your energy patterns and plan things around them so that you perform at your best when it really matters.

Chart your progress

Look back over the past six months and make a list of all your best achievements. They can be big or small, ranging from things like getting the stove door mended to making your presence known at work meetings or during question time after presentations.

Note down what you have learnt from these experiences and ways in which they have enriched your life. Have you managed to achieve something that you would never have imagined possible? That's what confidence can do for you.

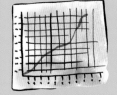

Accept criticism

Learn to handle criticism. Think about it: how many days go by without someone dishing some out? The trick is to think carefully before retaliating.

If the criticism seems unfair, stand up for yourself and say so. If, however, you decide it's justified (even just a tiny bit), and that they probably have got your best interests at heart, accept it and learn from it.

It takes confidence to admit that you are wrong or that you could do better, but you will feel all the stronger for doing it.

Instant confidence

BE A SHOE FUSSPOT

Polish your shoes and take any with worn-down heels or soles to be repaired. Neat feet will help your all-round confidence.

Desk-top confidence

A healthy desk promotes a healthy mind, so introducing order will make you feel more in control, as well as more confident about your work priorities.

Start by going through your bits of paper, filing them or throwing them away as necessary. Keep only work in progress on top of your desk. This will help to give you mental focus. From now on resolve to look at each piece of paper as it arrives on your desk. Either deal with it, file it or junk it.

When you are faced with a difficult situation see it as a challenge rather than a problem; something that is going to present ways for you to think about the meaning of your life and learn about yourself and others.

Adopting a positive rather than a negative approach like this can have a significant impact on how you feel about, and deal with, problems, helping you to react to them in a confident manner.

A smile is the shortest distance between two people.
Victor Borge

23 Think back

Sometimes you can find yourself in a situation where you feel scared and demoralized or worried about doing something for fear of failing. When this happens think back to similar difficult occasions when you have faced up to things and come out on top.

Make a list of at least ten things you have feared in your life and what the outcome was. Looking back like this can show you just how confident and courageous you can be and how much stronger a bit of backbone can make you.

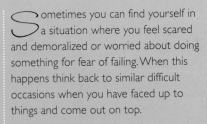

It's all very well making lists or talking big about the things you are going to do, but the important thing is to actually do them. So make sure you follow through any challenges you set yourself. These can be as big or as small as you like. For example, doing 100 lengths of your local swimming pool or making a cheese soufflé. As long as you see the task as a challenge, it counts.

What has this got to do with confidence building? Meeting challenges helps to reassure you that you are capable of translating what you say and think into confident actions.

25

Workspace makeover

Instant confidence

THE WHITE STUFF

A confident smile calls for pearly white teeth. Ask your dentist about teeth-whitening procedures so that your confidence can really shine out.

Check out the humidity level in your office. Low levels due to things like air conditioning can cause fatigue and dehydration, neither of which are good for your confidence levels. A simple solution is to distribute bowls of water, while upping the oxygen levels to boost mental clarity. Open the windows, if you can, and invest in some cheerful houseplants.

Confidence and creativity also come easier with sensory stimulation, so how about burning some uplifting essential oils, such as orange or peppermint, and hanging bright, stimulating pictures on the walls.

Know your limits

26

Confidence is about realizing your own limitations. For example, there is no point applying for a job requiring French if the last time you spoke it was at school. Why expose yourself to humiliation? Better to go for a job that you know you could be in the running for. It will lift your spirits.

Preparation matters

27

The key to success is self-confidence, and the key to self-confidence is preparation. This means you need to work hard to become confident. The more you do, the more you will achieve, and just as you feel confident in the presence of high achievers so your self-stature will increase.

28 | Find reassurance

An uneasy atmosphere at work can chip away at your self-confidence. So if you sense things are not quite as they should be, you need to get to the bottom of what could be wrong as fast as you can.

Find a colleague you can trust, with whom you can share your worries. Ask if they've noticed a strange atmosphere and if, perhaps, they know something you don't. Alternatively it could be something that you are doing but are not aware of, or it could be just you being paranoid. Reassure yourself or sort out the problem.

How about getting involved in one of the many fundraising challenges that are often reported? It's a great way of increasing your confidence while helping others at the same time. You could climb in the Himalayas, walk the Great Wall of China, trek through the Atlas Mountains or just sell raffle tickets or host a fundraising party. The size of the challenge doesn't matter. Big or small, you'll be helping others and yourself.

30

Start a lunchtime club

SPA OUT

Treat yourself to a day trip to your local spa. Chill out, get pampered, and you'll be sure to go home feeling on top of the world.

Does everyone at your workplace eat sandwiches at their desk or make solo trips down to the supermarket in search of lunchtime eats? Take a confident lead and suggest forming a lunchtime discussion club.

Pin invitations on the noticeboard and think of something really interesting to talk about. You'll forge new friendships, expand your knowledge in areas you may not have explored before and gain respect from your co-workers for showing such initiative.

If you are rejected by a potential employer or lover, dwell on it for too long and you risk damaging your self-esteem big time.

Instead of focusing on the negative angle, think of all the wonderful people who you have had a successful working relationship with, as well as the many people who love you and hold you in high regard.

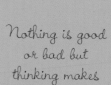

Nothing is good or bad but thinking makes it so.

William Shakespeare

Whether you tried out several ideas this month or just one, you might like to reflect on what you chose to try and why, and if it worked for you.

1. How many activities did you try this month?

- 1–3 activities ☐
- 4–10 activities ☐
- 11–20 activities ☐
- 21–31 activities ☐

2. How many did you repeat several times in the month?

- 1–3 activities ☐
- 4–10 activities ☐
- 11–20 activities ☐
- 21–31 activities ☐

3. Which activities had a positive effect on your mood this month?

Use the page opposite to make notes about what worked for you and what didn't.

Notes, jottings and thoughts

32

Date yourself

Identify six things you like doing and make appointments with yourself to do them regularly over the next six months. The more you fill your spare time with the things you enjoy, no matter how big or small, the more your confidence will grow. These could include spending time with your family, visiting art galleries, going to concerts or simply browsing around markets or second-hand bookstores.

Follow your own path, not someone else's. Look at your life and make sure you are doing what you really want to do rather than what your parents, friends or partner think is best for you. Stand your ground and do what feels right for you. Even if your nearest and dearest try to talk you out of it, don't be swayed. It is your life and if you lead it your way, the world will dance with you.

Insist on yourself; never imitate. Your own gift you can present every moment with the cumulative force of a whole life's cultivation; but of the adopted talent of another, you only have an extemporaneous half possession.

Ralph Waldo Emerson

34

Forget the past

Instant confidence

RING THE CHANGES

Do you tend to wear the same pair of earrings every day? Ring the changes and buy a couple of new pairs.

Today is the first day of the rest of your life. You can dump the past and start again. Now's your chance to shape whatever happens from now on and create a new, confident you.

Just because things have been a certain way till now, it doesn't mean they always have to be this way. You can change, you can be confident. It's up to you. So forget about past mistakes and failures. Whatever has happened before has gone for good.

> Men are disturbed not by things but by the view which they take of them.
>
> Epictetus

Try being kind to yourself today. And that means no under-the-breath comments such as 'I'm too fat', 'I'm so ugly' or 'I'm just useless and stupid.' You wouldn't pass verbal judgements like these on others, so why do it to yourself? Just stop it now. If you don't, they could become part of your automatic self-talk. Before you know it you'll be projecting a 'negative and useless' image to the world, and that is how others will see you.

36

Appreciate you

Feeling that you are never quite good enough and that everyone else is better than you can eat away at your self-esteem. Don't let it. Thinking that you never quite measure up or that you are not going to make it anyway is quite enough to scupper any chance of acquiring self-esteem.

Remind yourself about the things you have got and what you have done in comparison to so many others. You'll always know of someone who is better off than you in one way or another, but think about it, you have got something that they haven't. The secret is to keep things in perspective.

Start chatting to anyone you come across today and don't be choosy about who it is. It could be the cashier at the supermarket, the bus driver or your doctor's secretary. It doesn't matter; just strike up a conversation.

Sharpening up your social skills in your everyday life helps you to become more confident with people, especially people you don't know. As a result, you won't feel threatened or insecure in unfamiliar situations, especially at social events you find challenging such as parties or networking functions.

Buy a journal and jot down your feelings, ideas and thoughts every night before you go to bed. It will help to clarify your goals, build self-confidence and form a record that you can refer back to to see just how far you have progressed.

Keeping a regular journal will require a bit of self-discipline at first, but once you get into the routine you'll be amazed just how uplifting and confidence-boosting it can be.

When someone offers you praises or compliments learn to accept gracefully with a simple 'thank you' and a smile. OK, so it's easier to roll your eyes and shrug off the nice things people say about you, but think about it: all you are doing is feeding your unconfident self by reinforcing the belief that you are not worthy or deserving of praise. Stop it now!

> *You can't go around being what everyone expects you to be, living your life through other people's rules, and be happy and successful.*
>
> Dr Wayne W Dyer

40 Mend your ways

Bad habits can reinforce low self-esteem, especially if you know you should give them up but can't. Make a list and resolve to fix them one by one, setting a suitable time limit. So allow more time for stopping smoking than giving up playing computer games, skipping breakfast or not making your bed.

41 Think yourself confident

Think like a confident person and you will automatically feel and act more confidently. Take charge of your internal dialogue so that you always talk to yourself in an uplifting and positive way. Becoming a confident thinker is no more difficult than learning to ride a bicycle.

Make a list of at least five things you like about yourself. It could include patience, humor, kindness, intelligence or generosity. If you find yourself struggling to find five, think about traits you admire in your friends. What we admire in others is very often a projection of what we really like about ourselves, but won't admit to. Or ask a friend to list the five things she values about you. You could be surprised.

Add a new 'what I like about myself' item to the list every day and before you go to bed read the list out loud. Keep repeating it until you start to sound as though you actually believe in your likeable qualities.

Acknowledging what you like about yourself is a sure route to self-confidence. Visualize yourself as happy, poised and confident. Life is a self-fulfilling prophecy.

Instant confidence

TRY WHEATGRASS
Take yourself down to the local health food bar and ask for a shot of wheatgrass juice. It may not be the yummiest taste, but it's full of vital energy-giving ingredients.

43 | Be grateful

> We should be too big to take offence and too noble to give it.
> Abraham Lincoln

At the end of each day, jot down three things that have happened for which you feel grateful. Write as much or as little as you like about each item. As well as describing the positive event, explain why it happened. In other words, how did you make it happen?

It's a simple but very effective trick and this is why it works. By looking out for just three positive events a day, you get into the habit of recognizing what is going well in your life. You will start to notice many more positive events, exchanges and moments, which in turn will boost your mood and confidence.

Pick a restaurant you have always wanted to try, dress to kill and go for a meal by yourself. Don't let the waiters hide you away in a dark corner. Sit in full view of everyone and be proud to be solo. Take time studying the menu, select dishes that you haven't tried before and don't hold back on the wine. Go for a glass of the very best and enjoy it. At the end of the meal you will feel self-satisfied in more ways than one.

45 | Be good to others

React to others as you would like them to react to you. If you wait for others to behave in a particular way before you do so yourself you may well be waiting forever. For example, if you want someone to be affectionate toward you, make a point of being as affectionate as you can to them. You don't have to have a reason and don't expect any payback. Similarly, react to co-workers in the way you would like them to react to you. If they are rude or unfriendly don't automatically take your cue from them. It's up to you to set the tone yourself.

Close your eyes and think of a person you love and trust and who you know loves you. It could be your best friend, your sister or your lover. Think about all the things you adore and appreciate about this person, and notice how wonderful that love makes you feel.

Now turn it around the other way. Imagine you are your friend, sister or lover feeling that same deep love for you. Believe in this love and really feel it. Try to see yourself the way this other person sees you. Even if you can only do it for a moment you will experience a warm glow of confidence.

Instant confidence

GO FOR A KNUCKLE-DUSTER

Belong to the ring-on-every-finger brigade? One eye-catching knuckle-duster, which suits the shape of your fingers and hand, says more about your confidence than a ring on every finger does.

Make up your mind not to tell a single lie today, not even a little white one. Confident people are not frightened to tell the truth because they have nothing to hide and their self-belief is such that they are happy to face the music if it starts to play!

See if you can speak the truth for a day, then carry on the following day. Don't worry if you slip up, but don't give up. Just take a deep breath and start again.

Be aware the next time you feel really confident. It could be when you walk into a party feeling and looking a million dollars or the positive response you get after making a big presentation at work.

Make a mental note as to whether you were wearing a specific piece of jewelry at the time. Then next time you start to doubt yourself or feel a little insecure, all you have to do is call to mind this image, to remind yourself just how much you are really worth. Alternatively, wear that piece of jewelry when you want to feel confident.

49 Choose forgiveness

Instant confidence

**MASCARA'S
A MUST**

Make it a rule that you
never leave the house
without a slick of
mascara. You will appear
much more confident if
your eyes stand out.

This is easier to think about than
to do, but after an argument try
thinking about forgiving the instigator.
Choosing to forgive will help you to
understand the situation better.

By making a problem yours to forgive,
regardless of what the other person said
or how they behaved, you are instilling in
yourself a deep sense of confident control.

Like tends to attract like, so try to develop the qualities that you are looking for in other people. For example, the more you believe in and respect yourself, the more likely it is that others will believe in and have confidence in you.

The better you feel about yourself on the inside the more this will be reflected on the outside and to the world around you. Remember, to be confident you need to be your own best friend.

> The most profound relationship we'll ever have is the one we have with ourselves.
>
> Shirley MacLaine

51 Don't take the bait

Try to see the funny side of things and, more importantly, don't take yourself too seriously. If someone starts to bait you, try very hard not to rise to it. It's far better to laugh it off than to become defensive. Do that and your self-esteem will take a big knock.

Work on developing your sense of humor, then make a conscious effort to spend time with friends who enjoy having a good laugh. Having fun with like-minded people is one of the best recipes for lifting the spirits.

The only person who is really focused on you is you. Vow not to think twice about what others might think of you if you take up belly dancing, hula-hooping or dancing round the maypole. The important thing is to indulge your passions.

So, however eccentric your dream may seem, follow it. It can be incredibly liberating, building your confidence and self-esteem, and you may well be surprised by how little attention people really pay to many of the small things you are so worried about.

Live life to the full

Doing what you love to do is the secret to achieving super-confidence. Start by creating a project that excites you, regardless of what is going on at home or at work.

For example, if travel and adventure are important to you, plan an activity break rather than going for a sun-and-beach holiday. Or, if you want to inspire and lead others, volunteer to spearhead a project at work or offer to give a speech at a friend's birthday party or wedding.

By going beyond your own problems and taking care of others, you gain self-confidence, courage and a greater sense of calm.

Dalai Lama

Believe in yourself

54

If you want to succeed at something, then have faith in yourself. A good place to start is to visualize yourself doing what you want to achieve. For example, before making a speech a good confidence-boosting trick is to imagine yourself smartly dressed holding the attention of the audience as you speak out.

Don't be a doormat

55

Today put yourself first. Think twice before taking on responsibilities that should really be done by others. Think, is this task really my responsibility? Should someone else be doing it or helping me? Start asking others to do things for you. Remember, you are worth it.

56

Let it go

Instant confidence

HAVE A CLEAR-OUT

Go through your bookcases and make a pile of all the books that you are never likely to read again. Then take them round to your local thrift store. They will be delighted and you will feel unburdened.

Feeling resentful or full of regrets can really stand in the way of you becoming the confident person you want to be. Don't let this happen. Instead, find a quiet spot where you are unlikely to be disturbed, and call to mind someone you have unfinished business with. It could be a co-worker, a friend or an unrequited love.

Next focus on connecting with this person from the bottom of your heart and imagine yourself saying everything that needs to be said. To finish off, imagine yourself kissing them goodbye and walking away in full confidence that things have been sorted out, once and for all.

Knowing who you are and where you came from are essential parts of developing confidence in yourself. So start delving into your heritage. Begin by asking your parents to share with you all they know. Perhaps they have kept a hidden photo album or a bundle of letters that could enlighten you. Another source worth trying is your grandparents. Don't delay; get on the phone and book yourself in for a family history session.

'No matter what happens I can handle it.' Keep repeating this over and over again until it becomes automatic in your mind.

Susan Jeffers

Blow your own trumpet

There's nothing wrong with feeling smug occasionally. You might think it's arrogant, but even if you don't say it out loud, acknowledging to yourself what you are good at, and even things that you are most definitely better at than others, can boost your confidence wonderfully.

So, if you've just cooked a gourmet meal for ten, beat a friend at chess or sorted out a tricky situation at work, don't hold back from patting yourself on the back. Give praise where praise is due.

If you are one of those people who say, 'Oh, I'm no good at that, so what's the point of me even trying?' it's time for a rethink.

This is just negative self-talk; a sure sign of low self-esteem and fear of failure. It might feel more comfortable hanging on to these thought patterns, but if you want to walk the confident path, there's no place for thoughts like these. Instead, be bold and try your hand at whatever the day throws at you.

Change. It has the power to uplift, to heal, to stimulate, surprise, open new doors, bring fresh experience and create excitement in life. Certainly it is worth the risk.

Leo Buscaglia

60

Compromise, compromise

Instant confidence

SNACK SENSIBLY
Snack on dried fruits and nuts rather than chocolate or junk food for a long-lasting confidence boost. You may crave sweet things, but all you will get is a quick sugar fix that won't last long.

Saying 'no' to someone who wants you to do something can be very powerful, but it does not have to be unhelpful. You can always suggest a friend or co-worker who might be able to help out, or ask if they have considered such and such as an alternative.

You could also put forward a compromise such as 'I could do it for you next week when I am not likely to be so busy.'

If you get defensive in the face of criticism this is just the worst way of dealing with it. The most confident response, even if you feel the criticism is unjustified, is to say 'Thank you' graciously. It closes the conversation on a positive note and then it is up to you whether you pay attention to the cricitism or let it go. Asking yourself how you would feel if the same thing was said to someone else can help to put things in perspective.

A man's reach should be beyond his grasp, or what's a Heaven for?'
Robert Browning

checklist 2 *How did you do?*

Whether you tried out several ideas this month or just one, you might like to reflect on what you chose to try and why, and if it worked for you.

1. How many activities did you try this month?

- 1–3 activities ☐
- 4–10 activities ☐
- 11–20 activities ☐
- 21–30 activities ☐

2. How many did you repeat several times in the month?

- 1–3 activities ☐
- 4–10 activities ☐
- 11–20 activities ☐
- 21–30 activities ☐

3. Which activities had a positive effect on your mood this month?

Use the page opposite to make notes about what worked for you and what didn't.

Notes, jottings and thoughts

62

Sort it!

Instant confidence

LEARN THE ALEXANDER TECHNIQUE

Go sign up for some Alexander Technique lessons. You will learn how to strengthen the muscles that support your back, so much so that you'll soon find yourself walking the talk with no effort at all.

Been having a bad time at work and decided to move on? It will be much better for your confidence and your self-esteem if you don't leave under a cloud.

The key is to resolve whatever needs sorting before you make your exit. That way you will leave on a much more upbeat note and should find the transition into your new life that much easier.

Take a look around your home and ask yourself, 'Is this somewhere where I can really relax and recharge my batteries? Does it work for me? Am I happy with the layout, the furniture and the décor?' If your heart sinks, how about painting a wall a different color, changing the lighting, buying a new sofa, putting up some shelving or splashing out on some modern art?

Making a few small changes at home can make a big difference to how you feel about yourself. If the space you live in is positive and inspirational, you are much more likely to feel like conquering the world.

Fix it!

What's niggling you? Maybe it's that pile of ironing, the broken vacuum cleaner, the closet door that doesn't shut or the stove that needs cleaning. Make a 'to do' list of all the things that need fixing, select three of them and put a plan in action to get them sorted. Enjoy feeling the sense of achievement, then go back to your list and decide on a 'must-do-it-by' date for what still needs to be done.

The more things you sort out, the more positive the space around you will become and the better you will feel about yourself.

If you own things that hold unhappy memories for you, maybe now's the time to get rid of them. This may include presents from old lovers, jewelry, pictures, ornaments or perfumes that conjure up ghosts of long ago. They may have been expensive, but hey, that's the cost of freedom. Sell them if you can, give them to friends or family or donate them to charity. All these objects are doing is taking up space in your head and bringing down your morale every time you see them.

Confident decision-making is an attainable goal that simply requires practice. There is no magic involved in making good decisions.

Roger Dawson

Let there be light

Do you tend to feel more confident on a sunny day? Well here's the reason. As light enters the eye, it sends electrical impulses to the brain. These trigger the hypothalamus gland, which regulates most of the body's automatic functions, including mood. The more light there is, the more upbeat you are likely to feel.

So make sure that your home and your workplace are as light as they can be. If either is on the dark side it might be worth thinking about daylight bulbs or even investing in a light box.

According to Ancient Chinese wisdom, clutter represents blocked energy and can quickly dent your self-esteem. So have a good long think about what is cluttering your space, whether it's too much furniture, piles of old newspapers or clothes and shoes that you never wear.

Then try this formula: if something doesn't make you feel good about yourself or if you haven't used or worn it during the past 12 months, throw it out or give it away. You won't miss it.

68

Rubber gloves on

Even if you don't realize it, coming home to dusty surfaces and dirty windows can slowly chip away at your confidence. On the other hand, opening the front door to a bright and sparkling home can immediately lift your mood and make you feel a whole lot better about yourself.

So get out the vacuum cleaner, mop and duster and give your home a top-to-toe spring clean. If your home is really dirty get in the professionals to give it the once-over, then promise yourself you'll don the rubber gloves once a week from now on.

hrow mediocrity to the wind and don't settle for less than you are worth. Think big. What do you really want? A pay rise, a better job title, a promotion or just a more comfortable workstation?

Thinking big doesn't just apply to the workplace. Think about the rest of your life, too. Perhaps you want to have more sex with your partner, a different social life with your friends, a more upmarket house or to purchase a beautiful work of art. Dare to think about it. You are worth it. That's one of the first steps to self-esteem.

Instant confidence

GET UP THOSE STAIRS

Feeling stressed and low in self-esteem? Try running up and down the stairs a couple of times. You may get out of breath, but you'll feel a lot more confident about yourself.

70

Clear it!

Trying to get organized can be elusive and overwhelming. Choose a small space that needs attention such as a kitchen drawer. Throw out or recycle what you don't need, see to anything that needs attention and clean the drawer. You'll feel better and you will have created space for confidence to grow.

71

Be regular

Build routine into your life to give yourself a confident base from which to operate. List things to do on a regular basis, including, for example, going for a 30-minute morning walk, visiting the library weekly, reading a book monthly or having a night out with friends fortnightly.

Face up to obstacles

Life is full of obstacles at home and at work, but don't let them stand in your way of achieving what you want. If feelings of self-doubt start to creep in or the way forward seems hard to navigate, the secret is to act as if you are already well on the way to getting what you want.

Hold your head up high and carry on. You may not feel confident at the time, but you soon will. Bold behavior moves you forward, and your confidence will soon catch up with you. Best of all…the obstacles that seemed to be holding you up will fall by the wayside.

> Whatever you can do, or dream you can do, begin it. Boldness has genius, power and magic in it.
>
> Goethe

Every day has the same number of hours, but it is up to you how you spend them. It's all too easy to while away the hours and, before you know it, days, weeks and even months have passed and you have achieved very little.

The confident person uses a daily planner to chart the year. That way you can plan in key tasks, holidays, special events, birthdays, family occasions and regular meetings, and you can see at a glance how the next 12 months are likely to pan out. It is also a good way to keep a check on your goals and achievements.

Try using ingredients or seasonings from far-off places and build up your cooking confidence. Seek out some interesting ethnic markets and stores and start experimenting with different foods and tastes. There are plenty of recipe books on the market if you need inspiration.

Alternatively, study recipe pages in glossy magazines or tune in to a food show on TV. You will be spoilt for choice when it comes to planning next month's menus, and your friends will be queuing up for a place at the confident cook's dinner table.

75

Control it

> A journey of a thousand miles must begin with a single step.
>
> Lao Tsu

Rather than getting stressed about things that you can't change, put your energy into learning to control the things that you can. For example, getting on a bus during rush hour to go to do your shopping is guaranteed to take the smile off your face. Instead, take control and decide to do your shopping at a quieter time of day when there are fewer people about, or shop online. That way you avoid common stress-triggers and increase your chances of keeping your inner confidence intact.

Be ruthless and cut out activities and people that are a drain on your confidence and your energy: weekly clubs that have become a habit and that you no longer enjoy or get any benefit from; meetings that serve no purpose other than to lower your self-esteem; and friends or co-workers who constantly take from you without giving anything back.

Be polite but firm and remove these things from your life. That way you make space for confident people and more uplifting ways of passing your time.

77

Bliss out your bedroom

Instant confidence

LISTEN TO AN ARIA
You don't have to go the opera to benefit from its uplifting powers. Buy yourself some CDs, put on your earphones and get stuck in. Try Mozart's *Magic Flute* to get you started.

It doesn't take much to transform your bedroom into a haven where you can retreat for some feel-good, confidence-boosting relaxation. Treat yourself to a new bed and pile it up with pretty cushions and pure cotton bedclothes. Instead of harsh overhead lights, go for bedside lights and use soft-focus bulbs.

How about lighting candles occasionally, especially those made with pure essential oil? It's sheer bliss to fall asleep in a delicately scented room. Try ylang ylang, sandalwood or lavender essential oil in a burner, or put a couple of drops on your pillow. Be sure to use candles safely.

Learn how to put a new washer on a tap, mend a bike puncture and change a tyre. Knowing how to do these everyday things will boost your confidence on the DIY front and make you 100 percent independent. No need to rely on fathers, brothers and partners to come to your rescue or to make frantic calls to garages, odd-jobbers and pricy plumbers.

Buy a teach-yourself manual, go to an evening class or ask one of the professionals to show you how it's done.

> If you can't handle your neurosis, your neurosis will handle you.
>
> Chuck Spezzano

When scheduling time at home or in the office don't be over-optimistic about how long things take. If you only allow yourself two hours for a job that really requires three, you'll be rushing around to get it done in time and risk ending up annoying yourself (and everyone else!) if you don't meet your target.

It's far better to err on the generous side, then when you meet your deadline or, better still, get the job done early, your self-esteem will soar. Time-management experts recommend doubling the amount of time you estimate for any job.

Be enthusiastic

OK, so you don't really want to do the chores, but summoning up even a flicker of enthusiasm can bring in dividends. The housework, cleaning the car, weeding the garden or settling down to doing the filing may be boring, but put your best effort into all these things and you will experience a huge surge of confident satisfaction.

Enthusiasm is also infectious so, who knows, you may inspire someone else and even spur them into confident action.

Instant confidence

CLENCH IT

Clench one or both of your fists tightly, then release them gently. This will make you feel more relaxed, confident and in control of things.

Sort out your debts

Owing money on your credit cards or to friends and family can feel very debilitating. The bigger your debts, the bigger the potential drain on your confidence.

Restructuring your debts and making them more manageable is a good way to get back on track. Then you need to repay them gradually and to look at ways of curbing your spending habits. Who knows, you may get so good at it that you build up some savings for a more confident future.

Respect diversity

We are all different and our values and political views are shaped by our culture and experience. It's very likely that every day of your life you are going to come across individuals and groups of people who disagree with your views and beliefs. But, rather than allowing this to bring you down, respect their differing opinions and have confidence in your own. Try, also, to understand their outlook and where they are coming from, too.

We are what we think. With our thoughts, We make our world.

The Buddha

83

Change your time sheet

Have a lie-in once a week or maybe try to switch to flexitime at work. Offer to work on Saturdays and take a day off in the week. Varying your getting-up times and also your working hours can be very empowering.

Any break in your normal weekly routine you can make is a good thing, as it puts you firmly in the driving seat of your life rather than feeling that you are ruled by alarm clocks, time sheets and schedules.

Put crushers in their place

Have you noticed how some people seem to enjoy putting their friends down, saying that their ideas are pie in the sky? If someone tries to shatter your dreams, retaliation is what's called for.

The secret is to point out politely that you are not interested in negative comments and it's your call as to whether such and such an idea is worth pursuing. Then ask your critics if they wouldn't mind listening quietly to what you have to say before making any further comments.

There is only one journey. Going inside yourself.
Rainer Maria Rilke

Be amazing

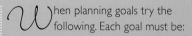

When planning goals try the following. Each goal must be:

- **Attainable.** You have to be able to achieve your goal with what you have already. For example, if you want to run a marathon, you have to be fit enough.
- **Measurable.** Make sure that anyone looking at your goal can understand it and will know when it has happened.
- **Accurate.** Make the image of your goal as specific and precise as possible so that there is no room for confusion.
- **Zoned.** This stands for 'time zone'. You must have a fixed date in your mind for completion of your goal.
- **Exact.** To get a clear image of your goal use all your senses to create it. For example, what it will look like, what it will smell like and what it will sound like?

Pick one thing that you are really good at and make up your mind to get better at it. It could be singing, acting, painting, gardening, cooking or even DIY.

Whether it involves joining a group, such as an amateur dramatics society, an evening cookery class or just spending time at home teaching yourself to paint, making the most of a talent can build confidence at a deep level. Better still, realizing that you are really good at something can make you feel much better about other areas in your life where you are less confident.

Stop the clock

Doing the same things over and over again soon takes its toll on your confidence levels and, before you know it, you are so down in the dumps that even the simplest exercise becomes a chore and an energy drain. Stop now and learn to just 'be'.

Do absolutely nothing. Just sit down or simply stop and stare. Try it for few moments at least three times today and every day. Forget your thoughts and worries and relish the empty moment for what it is. You'll find this helps to focus and calm you and keep your mood upbeat.

Bored with yet another night of predictable sex? How about perking up your sex life by trying out a few new positions?

It's easy to get into a sex rut out of laziness, but finding other ways to do it not only allows you to discover new sensations, but also gets you talking and laughing together.

You had better believe it…some positions are complicated and you need to spend time together working out how to do them. If you don't know where to start, buy yourself a sex manual and be inspired.

It is by having what we like that we are made happy, not by having what others think desirable.

La Rochefoucauld

89

Regret no more

It's time to bar phrases like 'If only', 'I should have' or 'Why didn't I?' from your vocabulary, now and forever. They have no part to play in the confident person's repertoire. If you start to utter them, replace them quickly with more positive words like 'Tomorrow, if I have the chance, I will.' Changing yesterday's regrets into today's goals means you are taking the first step on the road to achieving them.

Check out what movies are showing locally, pick one that you really want to see and go see it by yourself. This may sound easy enough to do, but it requires courage and, once achieved, will give your confidence no end of a boost. Do it and feel the pride well up.

Never again will you find yourself missing a movie because you have no one to go with. You will always be there for you.

Dare to branch out of your comfort zone. It may seem safe and cozy, but stay there and your confidence will stand still. Just taking one small step outside those inhibiting boundaries of security and under-achievement can be uplifting and liberating. But how do you take that step?

One way is to take a small but deliberate risk every day. Arrange a blind date, change the style of your hair, phone someone you would like to go out with and tell them so, or book yourself on a singles' holiday somewhere sunny. The more risks you take, the further your courage and confidence will grow.

Sort through old photographs and magazines and cut out any pictures, words and sayings that sum up what you want from life. Then get hold of a board and make your very own collage. Don't hold back. It doesn't matter how crazy and out of reach the images may appear, the important thing is to get them up there.

They could be pictures of your family, friends having fun, your dream car, fit and healthy bodies you aspire to, the latest catwalk designs, a beautiful sunset, your perfect house interior or even a signed IOU made out to yourself. All these things can inspire you and give you the confidence to go for what you want. Stick up your collage somewhere you can see it regularly.

Whether you tried out several ideas this month or just one, you might like to reflect on what you chose to try and why, and if it worked for you.

1. How many activities did you try this month?

* 1–3 activities ☐
* 4–10 activities ☐
* 11–20 activities ☐
* 21–31 activities ☐

2. How many did you repeat several times in the month?

* 1–3 activities ☐
* 4–10 activities ☐
* 11–20 activities ☐
* 21–31 activities ☐

3. Which activities had a positive effect on your mood this month?

Use the page opposite to make notes about what worked for you and what didn't.

Notes, jottings and thoughts

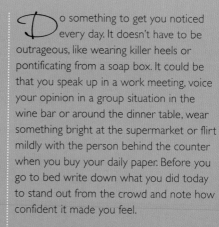

Do something to get you noticed every day. It doesn't have to be outrageous, like wearing killer heels or pontificating from a soap box. It could be that you speak up in a work meeting, voice your opinion in a group situation in the wine bar or around the dinner table, wear something bright at the supermarket or flirt mildly with the person behind the counter when you buy your daily paper. Before you go to bed write down what you did today to stand out from the crowd and note how confident it made you feel.

Feel the fear

Think about something you are nervous of doing in your day-to-day life. It could be making a speech in public, moving house or taking the plunge and telling your partner that things aren't as idyllic as they once were. Now's the time to put an action plan in place to get you on the road to achieving what you want. Start with small steps.

For example, if you want to move house, look in a few real estate agents' windows and make a couple of appointments to view some properties. Slowly try to come to terms with your own apprehension. As you do so you will become more and more confident in your action plan and will find the necessary support along the way to motivate you.

> Feel the fear and do it anyway.
> Susan Jeffers

95 | *Emotional wounds*

We all have things in our past which, although they happened years ago, can still bring up feelings of rejection and hurt. Now's the time to acknowledge them, because if you don't they will always get in the way of you becoming fully confident.

So cast your mind back over the years. It could be that your dad never turned up to your graduation ceremony, professing important business elsewhere. Or perhaps it's the time your best friend at school dropped you as soon as she went to college. It doesn't matter what caused the pain, but at least once acknowledged you can start to accept it and get on with the rest of your confident life.

If you make a mistake today or someone starts to criticize you, accept it gracefully. Admit your shortcomings and apologize. Resist the temptation to go into long rambling excuses as to why the mistake wasn't really your fault and that if you had had more time it would probably never have happened. Go down that route and all you are doing is opening yourself up to further criticism. It is far better to leave the explaining until later, when you are likely to be calmer and in a more confident mood.

Squeezing and contorting yourself to do something that goes against the grain is the biggest struggle you can give yourself.

Fiona Harrold

97

Create your own mantra

Draw up a short list of positive affirmations to repeat when your confidence needs a charge. You may need different affirmations for different situations. Imagine you have a personal coach beside you, motivating and encouraging you to do the best you can. Examples might include:

- Go on, you know you can do it!
- You've been here and got through it before.
- It's much easier than you think.
- Once you've done it you can relax.
- Think how good you will feel when it's all over.
- You are a money magnet.
- Well done, you're getting there!

Learn your affirmations by heart and repeat them whenever you feel the need.

Break out of your usual holiday routine. Rather than booking an organized trip, why not just get a flight somewhere new and see what happens when you get there. Or go for something more unusual, such as a yoga break. You'll meet new people and face new challenges. Be bold and get more confidence by trying out something completely different.

99

Listen up!

Instead of talking today, why not try brushing up your listening skills? Of course, you can't avoid talking completely, but you can try to keep the chat to a minimum and really focus on what others are saying.

Actively listening to somebody shows them that you value what they are saying. And when you show that you respect their opinions and thoughts, they will feel valued and loved and reciprocate these feelings to you. As a result, both of you will see your confidence levels rise.

How many times have you been told that there is no such word as 'should' and how many times have you ignored this advice? Well, today, try writing down the number of times you use the 'should' word and then think about whether these are things you really 'should' do.

For example, should you really work until six o' clock every night or are you just doing it because everyone else is? You will start to respect yourself a lot more when you remove the sense of obligation from your life and start to do things because you really want to.

> The minute you begin to do what you want to do, it's a different kind of life.
>
> Buckminster Fuller

101

Be in the here and now

Forget about there being a perfect moment for starting on that difficult project, joining that evening class or going abroad. What's wrong with the here and now? OK, it might not be exactly the start time you had anticipated, but it is infinitely better than sitting there doing nothing. Why?

The answer is because being in the here and now empowers you; it shows you are sitting confidently in the driving seat of your life and moving toward your goal. Learn to work with the here and now and you are well on your way to a confident new you.

Be clear and considered

If you are turning down someone because of a personal rule, tell them. It will help you to come across as a confident person who thinks before speaking. For example, if a friend wants to borrow money, saying 'I never lend friends money' shows that your refusal is an ongoing practice, to which you have given careful thought.

Sketch it

Have you had enough of making lists of confidence goals? Drawing engages the creative, right side of your brain. So get some pencils, a sketchpad and start drawing. Sketching a vibrant picture of your wildest confidence dreams encourages a 'sky's the limit' approach to life.

Change your tack

Instant confidence

....

PAY COMPLIMENTS

Why not pay a compliment to all those you meet today? The more compliments you give, the more you are likely to receive. Everyone wins.

To help you on your way to becoming the super-confident person of your dreams, start doing five things every day the way you imagine a super-confident person would.

For example, rather than mumbling your morning request for a hot cappuccino, look the guy in the coffee bar straight in the eye, say 'Hello' loudly and clearly and ask for your drink with a big smile.

Use the same tactics when you are buying your daily newspaper and bus or train ticket to work. You will be amazed by the positive reaction. Carry on like this and after just 25 days this attitude will have turned into a confident habit.

Just because you've always done something in a certain way at a certain time does not mean that it is necessarily the right way or that you can't do it differently. In fact, shaking up things can bolster self-esteem and new traditions are often born as older ones are discarded.

For example, if someone asks you for dinner on a Friday night, but you hesitate to accept because that's the night you go and see your parents, why not tell them you'll be round on Saturday instead? You will still be seeing them, but at a different time. You'll feel better about yourself because, at last, you are doing what you want on a Friday rather than slipping into a well-worn routine.

Be a dare devil

Always wanted to jump out of a plane, drive a powerboat or go white-water rafting? Now's the time to do it, however scared you feel!

Get that adrenaline going and you'll be fueling your confidence store. You'll also be opening yourself up to new challenges and feeling so proud of your own bravery that you'll be surfing along on a confidence wave for days afterward.

o you tend to complain about the lousy weather, the terrible state of public transport or the price of fuel? If you do, be careful; you'll immediately come across as a negative 'moany' person.

Instead, make a concerted effort to talk about the good things in your life, such as the new juice bar that just opened near your work, the wonderful massage you had last week or the lunchtime walks you look forward to in your local park. That way you'll come across as a confident person people will be pleased to have around, which is a great self-esteem booster.

What is this life, if, full of care, we have no time to stand and stare?

W H Davies

108

See things differently

Expanding how you view the world is a useful confidence-boosting exercise and an easy one to do. For example, if you enjoy reading why not join a book club? It will show you straight away that a story and its characters can be interpreted in more ways than one.

Then try reading a different newspaper to your normal daily broadsheet or tabloid, listen to the news on a different radio station or TV channel, and so on.

Change and confidence go together. The more changes you make and cope with successfully, the more your self-confidence will grow. But don't wait for things to change; set the train in motion by changing something small each day.

For example, you could start by getting up half an hour earlier, having something different for breakfast, walking all or part of the way to work rather than taking public transport and searching out some different lunch venues.

Even the smallest changes can add up over time and make you better able to cope with larger ones if and when they arise.

Act on feedback

There is nothing more boring than the undefeated. Any great, long career has at least one flame-out in it.

Tina Brown

After collecting feedback on what others see to be your strengths and weaknesses, look for common trends and themes and see if there are any you could develop further into goals. Pay attention to negative comments and either work on them to put them right or let them go, if this seems more appropriate.

But, remember, feedback is only someone else's opinion. The secret is to listen to it, take what supports you in building your confidence and let go of the rest.

Decide to see a funny play, movie or comedy show at least once a month. Comedy takes you out of your own little world and can help put things into perspective. Best of all, it will make you laugh, helping to increase your levels of endorphins, which are the body's own feel-good hormones.

Instant confidence

MAKE IT UP

Have a lesson on how to apply makeup to create your most confident look. Book an appointment at a specialist makeup counter and learn to put it on like the pros.

112 | Think before you leap

If you want to achieve your most confident and powerful version of yourself in the workplace, decide exactly what you want to get from your job. For example, promotion is always a powerful motivation, but is it what you really want? A fatter salary and greater prestige may well be on the cards, but can you hack the power and responsibility or will it quash your creative side?

Think carefully. If power politics is not your bag, the change could turn you from a happy, confident worker into an unhappy, less-confident manager. Do you really want that? If not, think about what would really make your work life better and go for that.

Be bold and voice your opinions in group discussions or put your hand up at question time in presentations. OK, you may feel terrified at first, but what is the worst that could happen? You could stutter over your words or get a few odd looks if the listeners can't quite grasp your point, but that's a risk well worth taking. Consider the potential confidence-boosting plusses of people sitting up, listening and even applauding your comments.

114

Be the first to speak

Do you want to appear the natural, confident leader in meetings? Try the following technique:

Make sure you are one of the first people to speak. As soon as you enter the room, say 'Hello' and make a comment, even if it is just to compliment one of your colleagues on a new hairstyle or the nice suit they are wearing today.

Try to come over as Mr or Ms charming. It will make others feel relaxed and you may find that people will pay attention to you much more, just because you have made the effort to say something.

Confident people steer well clear of those who whine or blame, or at least limit time spent with them. Hang around them for too long and, before you know it, you catch their way of thinking. Or worse still, your positive friends won't want to know you any more.

And this blame mindset is not the place to be if you want to succeed in the world. You just end up finding fault in others rather than taking responsibility for your actions.

Instant confidence

LOOK AFTER YOUR FEET
Go for a pedicure. Giving your feet some TLC can make you feel on top of the world and you'll walk better, too.

Be involved and engaged

As we let our light shine we unconsciously give other people the permission to do the same.

Nelson Mandela

When you are in meetings, listen to what is being said attentively and consider the outcome. That way you become more involved with the general discussion rather than trying to work out in advance what you need to say next.

Practice doing this and you will find that your comments are less contrived as well as more relevant and to the point. The result? You feel more confident.

Release tension and strain from your body by doing a few quick stretches when you get up in the morning. This will help you feel more confident at the start of your day.

Start by reaching above your head as far as you can with your fingertips. Then shrug your shoulders up and down from your ears, clasp your hands behind your back to release shoulder-blade tension and have a good yawn.

This series of movements increases oxygen flow to the brain, which in turn stimulates the production of endorphins, the body's own feel-good hormones. If you can't manage stretches, try clenching your fingers and toes, then gently releasing them several times.

The future belongs to those who believe in the beauty of their dreams.

Eleanor Roosevelt

If life gets too much, confidence drops. So what's the secret to keeping on an even keel? Avoid internalizing stress. A simple way to let it all out is to have a good scream. Find somewhere quiet and private, then open your mouth while tensing the muscles in your head and neck. Clench your fists, beat the air as hard as you can and scream to your heart's content. Relax, feel your muscles go limp, then repeat until you feel cool and calm.

Rather not scream? Laughing, crying or even thumping a cushion are just as good for releasing pent-up emotions.

To function at your most confident best, the secret is to balance doing too much with doing too little. If you are constantly on the run you just end up feeling out of sorts, which eventually affects your internal balance. Remember: 'busy-ness' does not always equal effectiveness.

Have a cat nap

120

Take an afternoon nap. It can have an amazingly restorative effect on your mood, increasing confidence as the day goes on. The best time to catch a few winks is early afternoon. Later and you may not be able to nod off at bedtime. Set an alarm for 20 minutes, close your eyes and snooze.

Go on a mini-break

It's within your power to get away from reality any time you like, but you need to train your mind to help you. Practice this exercise if you start to feel as though you are drowning in a sea of confidence-sapping self-doubt.

1. Close your eyes and take a few deep breaths. Create a mental picture of your dream holiday. Choose a really beautiful setting; it might be by the sea, in the mountains or in the forest.

2. Fill the scene with as much brightness and detail as you can. See the sights, smell the fragrances, hear the birds singing, the running water, the waves crashing on the rocks.

3. Focus on these vivid images for up to 15 minutes, then slowly let them go. When you open your eyes you'll be amazed how much better you feel.

Look at a map of the world. Let your imagination go wild and visualize yourself in beautiful faraway places, then narrow your choice to a couple of dream destinations. Switch your search to a travel company and find out how much a week's break would set you back.

Factor in costs for the flights, the hotels, meals and everything else you can think of. Then promise yourself that one day you are going to get there. And what better day than today to start planning your trip? Seeing the world helps to keep life interesting, broadens your horizons and can give the ego a boost like nothing else.

Instant confidence

TREAT YOURSELF
Get rid of any hand-me-downs in the closet from your sister, mother or cousin. You probably never wear them anyway. Pass them on to someone they might actually suit and treat yourself to a brand-new life-affirming outfit.

checklist 4 *How did you do?*

Whether you tried out several ideas this month or just one, you might like to reflect on what you chose to try and why, and if it worked for you.

1. How many activities did you try this month?

- 1–3 activities ☐
- 4–10 activities ☐
- 11–20 activities ☐
- 21–30 activities ☐

2. How many did you repeat several times in the month?

- 1–3 activities ☐
- 4–10 activities ☐
- 11–20 activities ☐
- 21–30 activities ☐

3. Which activities had a positive effect on your mood this month?

Use the page opposite to make notes about what worked for you and what didn't.

Notes, jottings and thoughts

123

Be touchy

Before you rush out to work or to do whatever you have planned for the day, give your partner, child or pet a cuddle. If you don't have any of these, then make sure you hug your friends and family at every opportunity.

Studies have shown that a simple loving touch can help to lower the stress hormone, cortisol, and encourage a surge of feel-good hormones, making the toucher and touched feel on top of the world. So a hug before a tough or busy day could help to relax you and keep you confident for hours.

Make time to go outdoors as often as you can. A walk at lunchtime, a leisurely visit to the local park or even a few moments in the garden or on your balcony all count.

Sunlight boosts levels of serotonin, the hormone that helps to keep you on an even keel, while communing with nature has an automatic grounding effect. It will help you to slow down, reconnect with the Earth and get things back into perspective.

Instant confidence

TRY IT ON

Have fun creating some confident new looks. Put on some loud music, get your clothes out of the closet and hold a fashion parade with yourself in front of a long mirror.

ollow in the steps of the ancient gurus of the East and massage away feelings of low self-esteem with some soothing acupressure. Try the following and see for yourself how you don't have to be an expert to give yourself an amazing confidence boost.

1. Find the acupressure point in the fleshy part of your hand, between your thumb and your forefinger, and press firmly down with the ball of your thumb or the tips of your fingers.
2. Hold for about 20 seconds, then let go slowly and gently.
3. Wait for ten seconds, before repeating the move up to five times more.

Check out hatha yoga classes or pilates sessions at your local gym. These two disciplines are both wonderful ways of strengthening your relationship with your body, helping you to understand and love it all the more. They are also relaxing and can help to ease any debilitating aches and pains you may have.

After just one class you can expect to feel the difference. And as you become more supple you will be able to hold your head up higher and keep your back that little bit straighter.

127 | Have a good day

Send your confidence levels soaring by deliberately choosing to have a good day. This means adopting a can-do attitude and putting your ball into play first, instead of always reacting to other people or letting others decide how things are going to go for you.

By being proactive, you make a conscious choice about the things you do and don't do. Think about what you can give to the world rather than what the world can give to you in return.

Try doing this for a week and you'll be amazed at how much happier and more confident you feel.

When work or family pressures get too much and start to take over your life, try this quick exercise to help keep you on the right side of confidence. You can do it anytime, anywhere, but start off by practicing at home for around 20 minutes a day to familiarize yourself with the moves.

Tense and relax all the major muscle groups in your body in turn. Start with your feet and work your way up your legs, buttocks, spine, shoulders, arms, hands, chest and abdomen, finishing with the muscles in your head and face. Focus on the difference in sensation between tension and relaxation.

Remember it's not where you've come from that counts, it's where you are going. Have fun along the way.

Fiona Harrold

Fire up some libido

HAVE A SING-ALONG

Go through your music collection. Out go all those painful dirge-like songs that signify unhappiness and low self-esteem. Replace them with strong life-affirming tunes and sing along to them at the top of your voice.

Refuel your sexual confidence by working out what makes you feel sexy and what first attracted you to your partner. If you are single think back to an important relationship and the qualities that you look for in a lover.

It could be their smile, their body language, their individual scent, their voice, the way they dance or their ability to make you smile. Whatever the attractions, write them down on a piece of paper and keep it somewhere safe. Then you can refer to it when you need reminding of what it feels like to be aroused.

We spend so much time thinking about the past and the future that we forget the present. Yet enjoying the here and now can help you develop a more confident inner self. Try going on a 'here-and-now' walk.

1. Go out and start walking; be aware of every single step.
2. While you walk see and smell the flowers, feel the wind blowing, watch the clouds, notice the houses and people, the dogs barking and birds singing. In the city be aware of cars, buses and people bustling.
3. If other thoughts creep into your head acknowledge them, but let them go and refocus on what's happening now.
4. After your walk, try to keep this new mindfulness with you for the rest of your day.

131

Build a nest

Just as birds build nests, you too will benefit if you create somewhere snug where you can feel safe, confident, warm and secure.

This retreat could be a room in your home such as your bedroom, your office or studio or the summerhouse in the garden. Just make sure you have somewhere where you can escape to regularly to relax and gather your thoughts.

If you really want to lift your sense of self-esteem, here's a good way to give it a boost.

Make a list of seven of your top strengths and then put one of them into practice every day for the next week. For example, if you choose tidiness, clear out some clutter. If you choose friendship, invite a group of friends round and cook them a delicious supper. If you choose kindness, ring up an elderly relative and offer to do their shopping for them.

Continue like this; one strength, one task a day, and by the end of the week you will feel on top of the world.

Get calm inside

Feeling calm inside is essential for an outward show of confidence. Write ten minutes of stillness into your journal and treat it as an appointment as serious as any other. Hang a do-not-disturb sign on your door and set your alarm for ten minutes.

Then try this meditation exercise. Simply focus on something simple like the flame of a burning candle in a darkened room or try clearing your mind and concentrating on a blue object, such as a painting or vase. Blue is a very calming color.

Be active in the sack

134

Don't take your sex life for granted, especially if you've been with your partner for a long time. Do it more often and you could see your confidence soar. When you climax, the feel-good hormone oxytocin surges through your bloodstream, leaving you feeling calm and confident.

Create a good-news club

135

Set up a good-news club with friends or colleagues. Meet once a month and make it a rule that you talk only about the good things that have happened. If negative comments do come up, try to see their positive sides and discuss ways you could turn them to your advantage.

136

Chill-out pose

Try the following yoga pose, known as the Reclining Cobbler, for chilled-out confidence.

1. Lie on your back, bring the soles of your feet together and relax your knees outward toward the floor.
2. Keep the heels of your feet toward your tailbone, inhale and lift your arms above and over your head on to the floor behind you. Keep your fingers interlaced and stretch your palms outward.
3. Close your eyes and take several deep relaxed breaths. You can stay in this position for up to ten minutes.

Do you need to gird your loins? This purple power breath is a right-now confident fix-and-a-half, according to the experts.

1. Sit in a quiet place and imagine you are surrounded by light that is a wonderful bright, clear imperial purple.
2. Breathe in for a steady count of five, taking it right down into your lungs, saying to yourself, 'I am breathing in power.'
3. Hold it for five, then breathe that glorious purple light out for five, saying as you do, 'I am breathing out strength.'
4. Repeat steps two and three five times (in power, out strength).
5. Now say to yourself, 'I have all the power and all the strength I need to be respected and heard.'
6. Stretch, open your eyes and have a quick glass of water.

138 | Lift it with scent

Indulging your sense of smell can help to lift your spirits. Why? The areas of the brain that process olfaction and emotion are closely linked, so the functioning of one area can have a direct impact on the other. After being exposed to a scent for about 20 minutes we no longer smell it, but the good mood remains.

Fill your house with sweet-smelling flowers, such as roses in summer and hyacinths in winter, or place aromatic candles in strategic places and let their perfume boost your senses. Alternatively, burn incense sticks, but make sure you keep an eye on them!

Adventure is the champagne of life.
G K Chesterton

Pat a pet

Boost your confidence in five seconds flat: stroke a cat or pat a dog. Time spent stroking and talking to animals increases endorphins, the body's own feel-good hormones, and decreases levels of cortisol, the stress hormone that can make you feel anxious.

If you don't have a pet of your own volunteer to look after someone else's for the day.

Every night, before you go to bed, make a mental list of the most important things you want to achieve tomorrow. While you are asleep, your unconscious mind will get to work on the best and simplest ways for you to achieve your aims.

When you wake up, think about your list again and decide how best to fit in your tasks to the time you have. If time looks as though it will be tight, leave out the least important. That way you start the day confident of achieving your 'to do' list, with a plan that will keep you focused on what really matters.

Trying to achieve perfection 24/7 will soon drive you and your confidence mad. It's OK to have dreams and goals, but if you strive too hard all the time the pressure can become unbearable.

Instead, keep your goals firmly in mind and put your best effort into achieving them. Aim as high as you can, but accept there will be occasions when you don't quite reach the summit.

Instant confidence

GO FOR A RE-STYLE

How long is it since you changed your hair? Why not try a new hairstyle every six to nine months? It's worth the risk and the good thing about hair is it always grows back again if you don't like the style.

Keep your confidence fired up with small, regular treats. You'll find that several small ones can sometimes be more effective than one big treat. They don't have to be exotic or expensive, but should have a feel-good factor.

How about a candle-lit bath in the evening when you get in from work, a chill-out in front of a log fire or a lovely long phone chat with an old friend?

Confident children thrive on praise, so get into the habit of praising your children not just for getting fantastic results but also for having a go in the first place.

This sort of encouragement will surely spur them on to do more and think better about themselves and their achievements. As their confidence improves, they will do better in everything they turn their hand to.

A side-effect of this strategy is that when you praise your kids for their strengths you will gradually notice that their faults become less of a problem.

Learn to spend time by yourself. A confident person is just as happy in their own company as they are in the company of others.

They know that time spent alone is essential for grounding themselves and getting in touch with who they really are. This enables them to operate from a point of maximum confidence for maximum effect.

Sex appeal is 50 percent what you've got and 50 percent what people think you've got.

Sophia Loren

Buy yourself a pretty notebook and write down any compliment or praise that you receive during the next seven days. Things like 'You look well today', 'I like your new haircut' and 'Your skin looks so clear' all count.

It's amazing how many compliments you can tot up over the week, but they are easy to forget. If you do something that you are pleased with make a note of it, too.

In future moments of self-doubt all you have to do is refer back to your notebook to see all the good things that people have said about you.

Instant confidence

WEAR IT WELL
Wear something different every day for the next week. Keep a record of how many compliments you get and watch your self-esteem grow.

146

Show an interest in friends

Ask your friends how they are and listen. Comment on their replies to show your interest is genuine. Treat everyone with respect, avoiding idle gossip and criticism. This makes you more worthy of trust and respect. Be discreet; your friends will treat you better, which will lift your self-esteem.

147

Please yourself

What do you really enjoy doing? Lazing in a warm bath, watching soaps, having a nap, chatting to a friend or reading magazines? Don't deny yourself such pleasures on the grounds that they are trivial. Confident people allow themselves small pleasures and you must, too.

Try to get your day off to a confident start with an uplifting wake-up shower. Alternating blasts of cold and hot water will kick-start your metabolism and boost circulation, encouraging oxygen-rich blood to reach every tissue in your body.

To continue the feel-good sensation, pat yourself dry with a thick, fluffy towel and moisturize your skin from top to toe. Use a body cream enriched with a few drops of peppermint or pine essential oil.

Get your beauty sleep

To function at its confident best your body needs rest, so make sure you get plenty of quality sleep. And here's why. It is during the night-time hours that the body goes through the essential processes of cell renewal and repair. Aim for at least eight hours' sleep a night and get into a regular bedtime routine.

Go to bed and get up at the same time each day, exercise and eat in the early evening, have a relaxing bath before going to bed and reserve your bedroom for sleep only. Yes, that really does mean no computer or TV in your bedroom.

Harness the power of essential oils and get into aromatherapy. It is thought that inhaling essential oils can help to influence your emotions, enhancing positive feelings such as confidence and relaxation. Mix oils with a carrier oil and use the mixture in your bath or shower, or put a couple of drops on your handkerchief and sniff at regular intervals. Look out for the following feel-good scents:

- Jasmine is heady and sweet and can produce positive feelings of confidence.
- Vetiver has a deep, smoky, earthy fragrance that is intensely calming and emotionally strengthening.
- Bergamot has a refreshing aroma that can be soothing in stressful moments.

Sexiness is a state of mind. It's about loving yourself in your most unlovable moments.

Halle Berry

159

Meditate, meditate

If you are feeling tired and frazzled, things can appear much bleaker than they really are. Try some meditation to bring back your inner equilibrium.

1. Find somewhere quiet. Sit or lie down. Draw the curtains or switch off the light to minimize distraction.
2. Close your eyes to help your brain to calm down and stop it processing information.
3. Breathe gently and focus on your breath as you inhale and exhale through your nose. If thoughts intrude, let them go.
4. Come to gently. Stay like this for five or ten minutes and gradually bring yourself back into the here and now by wiggling your fingers and toes and opening your eyes. Now slowly tune in to the world around you.

When did you last have a massage? Investigate beauty salons in your area and see what's available. Choose carefully and go for salons that promise an uplifting or revitalizing experience. Then book yourself in for a glorious hour (or more) of well-deserved self-indulgence and relaxation.

If you set aside some time out of your busy day to do this, you will feel good, and when you feel good, you'll feel more confident.

Whether you tried out several ideas this month or just one, you might like to reflect on what you chose to try and why, and if it worked for you.

1. How many activities did you try this month?

* 1–3 activities ☐
* 4–10 activities ☐
* 11–20 activities ☐
* 21–30 activities ☐

2. How many did you repeat several times in the month?

* 1–3 activities ☐
* 4–10 activities ☐
* 11–20 activities ☐
* 21–30 activities ☐

3. Which activities had a positive effect on your mood this month?

Use the page opposite to make notes about what worked for you and what didn't.

Notes, jottings and thoughts

153 | Try tapping

> Life is a daring adventure or nothing.
>
> Helen Keller

Emotional Freedom Technique, which involves a therapist tapping your body on specific energy points, is thought to help solve crises of confidence. Either book yourself in for a session with an expert or try the following exercise:

1. Using one hand, tap with the fingertips of your index and middle finger on one eyebrow six times, then on the bone under the eye six times and finally on the center of your collarbone six times.
2. Now change hands and try it out on the other eye.

Float away

Research carried out in Sweden shows that floating in a large dark tank of salted water could help to reduce stress and encourage feelings of confident optimism. The experience can be deeply relaxing, good for raising creativity levels and getting you going on inspiring ideas. It is especially good for getting you out of a rut.

So if you feel stuck in an unconfident place, why not give flotation a go? Look on the Internet for a tank located near you.

Instant confidence

PULL ON THE FISHNETS

Try fishnet pantyhose to show your legs off to their best advantage and play down your frumpy side. Bring out your sexy and confident self for a change!

155 | *Check your cycle*

Do you feel as though your confidence levels are a little shaky? Well, how about checking your calendar? If it's between 14 and 28 days since your last period perhaps this is the reason why.

High levels of estrogen make the right emotional hemisphere of the brain more active after ovulation, which makes you more likely to pay attention to self-deprecating thoughts, says Dr Mona Lisa Schulz, author of *The New Feminine Brain*.

Simply knowing this can help reduce the power that negative thoughts may have over you. But if they persist, try repeating the word 'cancel' to yourself at least 20 times to help switch off negative thoughts.

Buy a special notebook and each evening write down particular sensations that have brought you joy today. It could be the scent of a bunch of freesias in the flower shop, the cheerful noise of children playing in the park, some music you heard on the radio or simply the smell of freshly baked bread.

Really visualize, taste or smell the sensations as you put them down on paper. Keep this list somewhere handy and carry on adding to it. Revisit it whenever you need some good vibes to get you through the day.

157

Get local

Becoming personally involved in your local community can be empowering. The good news is that doing so can make a genuine difference to your neighborhood.

So look around you for a special cause you would like to support. It could be preventing cell phone masts being erected on the hill opposite your home or putting a stop to that huge apartment block that would become an eyesore in the next-door road.

Ring up your girlfriends and arrange to go out for a night on the town. Eating a delicious meal, chatting and sharing a good bottle of wine can work wonders for your confidence and wellbeing. Why?

You'll be doing something you like doing, with people you like being with, who in return make you feel worthwhile and good about yourself. So why not book that Friday night out now!

159 | Be a child

Do at least one playful thing today and see how much it nurtures and strengthens you.

Try recreating some of your childhood experiences: build a mud pie, climb a tree, suck a lollipop, catch some floating leaves, slosh around in a puddle or buy some bubbles and have fun blowing them.

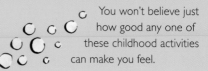

You won't believe just how good any one of these childhood activities can make you feel.

Love your job and you will find that you'll be able to act from a confident place. If you hate it, your boss or your co-workers puts you at odds with your deeper self-beliefs and values.

Your self-esteem will also suffer, as you are hardly likely to be yourself if you are in a job you don't like. So, if you are unhappy at work, now might be a good time to consider your work plan and think about what you really do want from your career.

Turn the music on

> Each human being has the potential to change, to transform their attitude, no matter how difficult the situation.
>
> Dalai Lama

Change your mood from negative to positively confident with a spot of music therapy. The key is to work out exactly how you feel and gradually shift your mood with a careful choice of tunes.

If your morale feels a little low, start with something soft, slow and soothing, then follow with a more uplifting tune. As a grand finale try something that will really rouse your spirits. 'The Hallelujah Chorus' from Handel's *Messiah* is always a good choice. Use a personal stereo so that you can plug into this instant confidence-booster wherever you are.

Don't wait to go to a dance class to reap the feel-good benefits of dancing. If you need a quick confidence fix you can always put on your favorite music and get moving right here and now.

Play something with a strong rhythm and let your body leap, bend, twist and spin to the beat. Do whatever comes naturally to you rather than moving in a specific way.

When you have had your fill, simply lie down on the floor for a few moments to let your heartbeat slow down and enjoy the quiet feeling of confidence that starts to flood through your body.

Instant confidence

MAKE DETAIL MATTER

Paying attention to detail can make all the difference. A chic, confident outfit can be completely ruined by chipped nail varnish or a hole in your sweater.

Shake up your sex life

> If you head towards your goal with courage and determination, all the powers of the universe will come to your aid.
>
> Ralph Waldo Emerson

In the same way that refreshing your exercise routine every few months can make for more body-confidence, so can revamping your sex life. Start by thinking about how you would like to spice things up. What would make things more upbeat? Spontaneous sex? Sex in the bath? Sex in the garden?

Be adventurous. Surf the Internet for ideas, read magazines, ask trusted friends for advice. Then set aside an afternoon when you and your partner have plenty of time to play, and start living out your fantasies.

Expect it and get it

Be careful what you wish for because it might actually happen! The same applies to what you think. Unconfident thoughts may lead to you acting unconfidently. But if you want positive, confident outcomes then positive, confident thoughts may bring results. So expect good things to happen to you!

Get real

Stop thinking that if you lost weight everything would be different. This thinking will never lead you to body-confidence; you will always be waiting for the unlikely to happen. Far better to accept that your body is great the way it is, but what a bonus if you did lose a few pounds!

166 Look after yourself well

Self-nurture plays a big part in building self-confidence. Don't see it as selfish, but rather as a self-improving exercise. Aim for 30 minutes of self-nurture a day. Here are some ideas to get you started.

- Go for a coffee at your local coffee bar.
- Curl up and read the latest bestseller.
- Go for a bike ride.
- Do some yoga or simple stretches.
- Take a long, luxurious bath.
- Go for a run or a brisk walk.
- Try on all your clothes and improvise new ways of putting them together.

Add more '-ing' to your life, for example running, hik-ing, cook-ing, paint-ing. Do-ing things you enjoy will make you happy, vital and confident.

Karen Salmansohn

Think of something you would like to do but don't because your nerves always get the better of you.

Repeat over and over again that you know you can do this thing and that you will. Then find yourself a quiet place, sit down, relax, close your eyes and spend a few moments visualizing yourself doing it with masses of confidence.

Hold the picture firmly in your mind, before slowly opening your eyes. Then be brave, go for the nerve-wracking experience and enjoy the buzz and feeling of achievement it brings afterward.

168

Stop low self-esteem

Instant confidence

DRESS FOR YOURSELF
Today you are going to dress to feel attractive to yourself. Forget everyone else, just for once. You will be surprised; others will notice and feel attracted to you, too.

Stop unconfident, low self-esteem thoughts in their tracks. As soon as you start to feel them coming on, don't hesitate. Don't allow yourself even a moment to wallow in them.

That means no sitting there staring at the wall or, worse, gazing into space. Get up and do something. Go for a walk, start writing or reading, put the washing on, get gardening… anything that makes you active. You are in control of your thoughts, so don't let them run away down the negative path.

Often the first steps are the hardest. So, look up the number for the phone call you have to make and write it down, put the files on your desk for the project you have to plan, search for dating sites on the Internet and bookmark them.

Sometimes just making a start on something and showing yourself that you are serious is all you need to give you the impetus to get going on a difficult project.

Concentrating on the first, easiest thing rather than the scope of what lies ahead makes a thing do-able. You will feel a huge sense of relief.

Make the most of yourself, for that is all there is of you.

Ralph Waldo Emerson

Calm down

This yoga pose, called Legs Up the Wall, calms your nervous system and leaves you feeling relaxed and refreshed.

Lie on your side in the fetal position, with your feet a short distance from a wall. Roll onto your back and swing your legs up against it. Straighten your legs and inch your buttocks in toward the wall. Lie quietly in this position, breathing deeply for as long as it feels good.

eeling uptight and low in self-esteem? Look down at your body. You'll probably find that it's all tensed up. Try the following simple moves to loosen yourself up.

- Unclench your fists and let your hands hang loose by your sides.
- Uncross your arms and legs.
- Rotate your ankles first one way, then the other.
- Shake your arms and legs as vigorously as you can.

Instant confidence

THINK AHEAD
Take lots of photos of your new, confident self to remind yourself in 20 years' time of how great you look today.

181

Change the way you think

Finding it difficult to alter the way you think? A short course of cognitive behavioral therapy (CBT) might be the answer for you. The theory behind this therapy is that many of us get stuck in unhealthy patterns of behavior because of faulty thinking.

CBT teaches you how to challenge these thoughts by asking questions such as 'Does it make sense?' and 'Where is the evidence for this thought?' and coming up with a more rational way of dealing with the situation.

For example, if you are unhappy in your job you would be encouraged to ask yourself questions like 'Does it make rational sense to stay in a job I hate so much?'

Success is getting what you want. Happiness is wanting what you get.

Dale Carnegie

*F*ocus on three areas that work in your life today rather than dwelling on the things that don't work so well.

For example, if you love going to yoga class, then book a weekend workshop; if you love reading, then buy yourself two new novels; if you love going to the movies, then form a movie group with a couple of friends and make Friday nights movie nights.

Instant confidence

BE THANKFUL
Instead of focusing on the things you haven't got, switch your thoughts to all the wonderful things you have been blessed with.

Put the pressure on

Shiatsu, the ancient Japanese massage technique, which uses firm pressure on certain points of the body, can help you to stay calm and confident as well as full of energy. Try out a few sample sessions with a professional practitioner or try the following simple moves at home.

1. To achieve relaxation, grasp your foot and use your thumbs to press the point between the two pads of your sole. Firmly rotate both thumbs.
2. To boost energy, grasp your foot and pull each toe gently apart from the one next to it. Hold and massage in the web of flesh between each toe, using your thumb on top and your forefinger underneath.
3. To ease anxiety, use your fists to drum lightly in all directions across the top of your head.

Feeling drained of every drop of energy with your confidence hitting rock bottom? Then treat yourself to a guilt-free day off under the covers.

You can read that unfinished novel that's been beside your bed for months, ring up friends and family, watch TV or DVDs, listen to music and eat your favorite foods. Alternatively, just lie there and relax. You'll feel all the better for it tomorrow.

176 *Accept yourself*

Maybe you think your nose is too long or your bottom too big, but do you notice such things when you meet new people? Probably not. Even if people do see your 'defects', it's not going to change their opinion of you fundamentally. So be confident and love yourself just the way you are.

177 *Step into their shoes*

It's a generous move and one that can be very hard to do, but if you find yourself on the edge of confrontation with a friend, step into their shoes for a moment. Seeing what the situation looks like from their perspective can throw a whole different light on the situation.

I t's all too easy to focus on what your body can't do rather than thinking about the successes it has contributed to your life.

Now's the time to draw up a mental inventory of everything your body has achieved for you to date. This could be anything from passing your driving test to overcoming an illness, giving birth or even perhaps running a half marathon.

And don't stop there. Think about all the things you want to achieve in the future and how you are going to get there. Forming a positive body image of yourself in your mind can be incredibly empowering, leading to greater personal confidence.

Instant confidence

PAINT THOSE TOES
Put some sparkle on your toenails. A striking red conveys confidence and a pretty pink quiet self-assurance.

Nothing says 'I lack confidence' more than someone who looks as though they are trying to hide from the world; their body speaks of their lack of confidence.

So don't slouch or slump your shoulders. Instead, keep your back straight, your shoulders square and lowered and your chest puffed out slightly (but stay loose, otherwise you'll come across as stiff and uptight). Keep your chin up and your eyes forward. Remember, the ground is not for looking at.

Never bend your head. Always have it high. Look the world straight in the face.

Hellen Keller

If you tend to store tension in your head try this scalp massage to ease the strain. Find your hairline and, using four fingertips of both hands, press your forehead for a couple of seconds, then release. Repeat the circuit two or three times. Finish off by pressing your fingertips into the crown of your head. It takes just a few seconds and, best of all, the uplifting benefits are instant.

181 Talk body language

HAVE A FACIAL
Treat yourself to a facial
at your local beauty
salon every couple of
months. It will keep your
skin glowing and vibrant
and leave you feeling as
though you are on top
of the world.

There's no need to be confident to start using confident body language. When you meet someone or walk into a meeting room, the key is to straighten your back, keep your head up high and look directly at the person you are talking to. Although you can't see yourself, you will instantly appear more confident.

Smiling is another important thing to do. Force one, even if you feel like death. It works like magic in the 'I'm so confident' approach! Be conscious of your body language for three weeks and after nine weeks it will become a habit.

Play footsie

Reflexology is a natural confidence-booster. This ancient therapy involves the manipulation of certain points or reflexes on your feet. It uses firm pressure rather than light movements, so don't worry, it won't tickle you. You can either book a session with a professional or, if you are after an instant confidence charge, try the following at home:

1. Find the reflex point at the base of the ball of your foot, just below your big toe (it relates to your adrenal glands).
2. Using your thumb or finger, push down steadily and, keeping the pressure on the point for around 30 seconds, 'walk it' by moving your wrist up and down. It may sound difficult, but with practice it will become second nature.

Whether you tried out several ideas this month or just one, you might like to reflect on what you chose to try and why, and if it worked for you.

1. How many activities did you try this month?

- 1–3 activities ☐
- 4–10 activities ☐
- 11–20 activities ☐
- 21–30 activities ☐

2. How many did you repeat several times in the month?

- 1–3 activities ☐
- 4–10 activities ☐
- 11–20 activities ☐
- 21–30 activities ☐

3. Which activities had a positive effect on your mood this month?

Use the page opposite to make notes about what worked for you and what didn't.

Notes, jottings and thoughts

183

Be a naked ape

*Try a thing
you haven't tried
before three
times: once to get
over the fear,
once to find out
how to do it,
and a third time
to find out if
you like it
or not.*

Virgil Thomson

Stand naked in front of a mirror and take a long, hard look at your body. Start to notice all the things you love about it. Look at you arms, your legs, your skin, your teeth, your eyes, your ankles and, yes, even your bottom. Yes, you do have assets, so start to appreciate them.

Stand up straight and, looking yourself in the eye, state out loud all the things that give you pleasure about your body. Do this often and you will soon discover that as you start to have confidence in your body, others will, too.

Whether you are having a difficult conversation with your partner, giving a presentation at work or a speech in front of an audience, shifting your weight to the balls of your feet can make you feel far more confident.

Other quick tricks include pausing to collect yourself before you start talking (the wait can make you appear more sure of yourself) and maintaining your pace, even as you build up to making your main point.

Instant confidence

HUM HUM
Try humming to alleviate low-mood feelings. It causes relaxing vibrations in your throat, which in turn can boost confidence levels. A word of warning: take care you don't stress out others with your humming.

185

Seeing it differently

> There ain't a lot of fun in medicine but there's a heck of a lot of medicine in fun.
>
> Josh Billings

Imagine you are one of your friends describing your body to someone else, then write down the description, being as accurate and honest as you can.

If you are looking at yourself through another's eyes you may well be a lot less harsh on yourself than you would be if you were looking through your own eyes.

Try to use this more realistic judgment when casting a critical eye on yourself. It is, after all, how the rest of the world probably sees you and, once you realize this, you'll feel more confident about your body.

If you're feeling sluggish and your body image is on a downward spiral a daily session of skin-brushing can really perk things up for you.

Using a hemp glove or a long-handled, natural-bristle brush, sweep smoothly up your legs. Then move on to your buttocks and lower back, always working in the direction of your heart.

Now brush the front and the back of each hand, up your arms, across your shoulders and down your chest. Do your abdomen last, with clockwise, circular movements. The routine should take around five minutes; as long as it takes for you to run your bath.

187

Love your bits

> If you hear a voice within you say 'You cannot paint,' then by all means paint, and that voice will be silenced.
>
> Vincent Van Gogh

Choose a part of your body that you like. It could be your hands, your feet, ankles or even your big toe. Then tell yourself loudly and clearly what it is about this body bit that you like.

This approach immediately shifts your focus from the areas you don't like, helping you to see your body as a whole rather than as a collection of isolated parts. As a result, you will feel more body-confident and will start to use your body in a more positive way.

How you make your entrance into a room can make all the difference to how confident you feel on the inside and look on the outside. Try this trick, used by teachers of the Alexander Technique.

As you walk through the door, straighten yourself up and stand tall, as though your head is suspended by a hook attached to the ceiling, and your feet firmly planted on the ground with roots growing down. Then concentrate on pulling yourself up through the middle of your body.

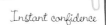

Instant confidence

PHONE A FRIEND
Ring your most confident friend and hang on to every word she says. You'll catch her vibe and experience a big surge in your own confident feelings.

189 | *Pose naked*

Be brave and offer to pose naked for an artist friend (or offer yourself as a model to a life class). Either strip off or put on a bikini, then ask your friend to draw you as you pose.

Next swap positions and draw your friend in the nude. Notice, as you draw, how you look at her body without critical judgment. Share your drawings with each other and see your body through another's eyes.

Recall this exercise next time you start to obsess about your own body 'faults'. No one is ever as critical of your body as you are.

Man's mind stretched to a new idea never goes back to its original shape.
Oliver Wendell Holmes

It's true that you can't stop getting older, but there is plenty you can do to make each decade a confident, positive period in your life. The secret about coping with the inevitable changes that come along as you age is to accept the things you can't alter and change the ones you can.

For example, you can wear plenty of sunscreen to minimize wrinkles, eat lots of fish to help fight heart disease, take calcium and vitamin D to strengthen your bones and exercise regularly to boost your energy levels and keep joints supple.

To be truly confident you need to be physically mindful. But all too often we live in our heads and only become really aware of our bodies when something starts to hurt or we catch sight of ourselves in a mirror and don't like what we see.

Start being body-mindful by asking yourself which part or aspect of your body holds the most of your tension? Which part is the strongest, most supple or vulnerable to injury? Think about the care and attention your body needs to be able to function at its confident best, then start to look after it.

Do something normal. This could be phoning a friend or making a cup of coffee, but without your clothes on. Going naked can make you feel unbelievably confident as well as putting you at ease with your body.

But stay away from mirrors while you do this one. You need to focus on your inner confidence rather than on areas of your body that you are less than happy with. Catching sight of your naked silhouette could make you self-conscious, which would just defeat the object of the exercise.

193 Ask a friend

Instant confidence

EMBRACE LIFE
Put some effort into your life today. Remember you are the creator of your life and the more you engage in it the more confident you will become.

Invite your best girlfriend round and try this body-image-boosting exercise. Ask her to list three things that she likes about your body. It could be your wonderful big eyes, the shape of your nails or even your lovely curly hair. It doesn't matter if you don't agree with her! After each statement pause for a few moments before saying a simple 'thank you'.

Really think about and try to appreciate each compliment rather than dismissing it with a negative thought such as 'what is she talking about?' Although it may seem too easy to be true, this exercise will leave you feeling good, with a positive, confident image of your body.

See it for real

Looking at magazines full of stick-thin models is a sure-fire way to make you feel inadequate, especially if you are trying to lose weight. Remember, the models may have been airbrushed and probably spent hours in hair and make-up. Real people don't look like this, so try to keep a sense of perspective.

Open up those shoulders

Hunched shoulders don't do much for body-confidence. If you work at a computer for hours on end, do this simple stretch regularly to open up your shoulders. Sit forward and link your hands behind your body, drawing your shoulder blades together. Hold for 10–30 seconds.

196 | Tweeze it!

*N*ever underestimate the power of a good eyebrow shape. It can help lift your self-image as well as your face and take years off you. How good is that for self-esteem? For the best results go to a beautician who specializes in eyebrows or visit an eyebrow bar. They'll create a great shape you can work with, and you can then pluck out any re-growth as it comes through yourself.

Want to come across as organized, positive and confident? It could be time for a handbag detox. If yours is bulging and overloaded there may well be other areas of disorganization in your life, not to mention your head!

So have a good clear-out. Throw away scraps of paper, old shopping lists, receipts, movie tickets and pens that don't work. Banish any lurking bits of old makeup and put all your current items in a small, neat cosmetic bag.

> Invent your world.
> Surround yourself with
> people, color, sounds and
> work that nourish you.
>
> Sark

The following exercise will help you to present a confident, relaxed face to the world.

1. Place the tip of each index finger on the inside edge of each eyebrow (the bit closest to the bridge of your nose).
2. Using the muscles under the skin just below your third eye (the center of your forehead) move the ends of your fingertips slightly apart.
3. Hold for a count of ten, then gradually release.
4. Repeat three times, twice a day.

Emotions rise and fall all the time, from happiness and love to anger and sadness. And if you are on the volatile side you need to get in tune with these moods rather than fall victim to them. Feeling in control will really help to boost your confidence.

Although you may not realize it, your inner feelings can show as much through your expressions and gestures as by what you do and don't say. If you know you are not in the best of moods, then it's probably not the right time to make decisions.

Instant confidence

TRY KARAOKE
How about trying your hand at karaoke? This is your chance to shine in front of others. Take the risk and enjoy the spotlight. It will make you feel exhilarated.

People form an opinion within the first 15 to 20 seconds of meeting you. So be sure not to leave the house without first checking yourself from top to toe in a full-length mirror.

Watch out for food marks on clothes, ladders in tights, holes in sweaters and scuffed shoes. Yes, they do matter!

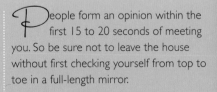

You must first be who you really are, then do what you need to do in order to have what you want.

Margaret Young

If you put off doing something until you are absolutely certain that it is the right thing to do, the chances are that it will never come to be.

Try to get comfortable with 80 percent certainty, reminding yourself that the only really certain thing in life is uncertainty. You'll soon get used to a little bit of it in life and confident people know it's all part of the moving-out-of-your-comfort zone process.

Instant confidence

TRY SPEEDWRITING
Set a timer for five minutes and write down as much as you can about what you have achieved today.

Get to it!

Action builds confidence. Even the smallest bit contributes to the powerful confident belief, 'I can.' Inaction, or 'standing still', however, has the opposite effect. It erodes confidence, even sometimes in areas where you once had it.

Start by taking decisive action in one small area of your life. For example, if you are trying to lose weight it could be something as simple as giving up sugar in your tea. Even the smallest achievement will make you more confident when it comes to facing up to larger challenges.

It is tempting to arm yourself with a plate of food at a party, as it gives you something to do, but just as animals give one another a wide berth when they are eating, so do humans.

You may also find yourself offering to take round the canapés because you haven't got anyone to talk to, but although you will be saying 'hello' to a lot of people, it is unlikely to lead to confident conversation. Your body language is saying 'I am busy' and most people won't engage with you for long.

Be briefcase-confident

Organize your briefcase so that your important notes are divided up into separate folders rather than placed all together in an embarrassing heap. You don't want to have to shuffle through your briefcase at the beginning of a meeting as it will make you look more disorganized than you really are.

Also, when traveling on business, opt for smart classic luggage with plenty of compartments. That way you'll avoid personal belongings spilling out of your briefcase as you take out your laptop or files.

Do you 'pitter patter' with girlfriends and sisters in the following manner: 'Look at my tummy, it's so fat, and I've got these rolls on my back. And then there's my double chin and the bags under my eyes.' If this sounds like you, it's time to stop, right now. Putting negative body-image thoughts into words somehow makes them real and sharing them with friends merely reinforces them; that's anathema to self-confidence.

So let your friends know that you've had enough of negative self-talk and instead will be shouting about your positive strengths… and theirs, of course, as well.

Saying 'yes' and 'no' clearly builds confidence and rids us of the misconception that we are powerless.

Marsha Sintar

206 Make a positive reply

Your only obligation in any lifetime is to be true to yourself.
Richard Bach

Try to respond to any questions positively. One of the first questions most people ask is 'How are you?' The usual answer is 'fine' or 'OK'. Answer more positively with 'I'm great, how are you?' and you'll create a confident impression with the other person, making you both feel good about each other.

207 De-clutter your head

Positive lists are great for triggering confident thoughts, but sometimes it can be hard to tap into that positivity. Try writing a list of thoughts that you would like to rid your head of. Writing down unhelpful thoughts can make room for more creative, life-affirming ideas to emerge.

Do you revisit negative themes about yourself, such as: 'I'm too fat, too plain, ugly and stupid'. Sound familiar? If you answer 'yes' you've probably received negative messages such as these in your early years. Now's the time to put them firmly to rest.

First identify from where or whom your negative impressions about yourself stem. Then write 'I no longer need to believe my mother/father/teacher's thoughts about me. I am my own person and choose to see myself as confident, dynamic and attractive'.

Write out this personal mantra several times every morning and evening (when your subconscious is at its most receptive). Do it for a month and you will have reprogramed your brain to think confident, positive, life- enhancing thoughts.

Instant confidence

CAPTURE THE PICTURE

Take a photograph of somewhere or something that conjures up your confident future and use it as a screen grab on your computer.

Change your mind

CLEAR THE AIR
Invest in an ionizer to remedy poor air quality, clear the atmosphere and boost confidence.

Challenging long-held beliefs can be liberating and uplifting, and can give you a push on your confidence journey. Try this exercise and discover just how good a confidence challenge can be. Write down a list of beliefs you hold about yourself and the world around you. Then ask yourself:

- How many of these beliefs could be founded on misinterpretations?
- Are they actually someone else's opinion or my own?
- How many of the beliefs are no longer useful or relevant to my life?
- Now cross off your list five key beliefs that have limited you in the past and replace them with five new ones. Pin them up where you can see them.
- Repeat this exercise at regular intervals.

Using different words and phrases for things you don't like doing can turn them from negative to positive experiences, which in turn can help to boost self-esteem.

For example, instead of dreading that dull Monday-morning meeting, think of it as an exciting brainstorming session. You'll be much more likely to come up with bright ideas and your positive, confident energy will rub off on co-workers, too.

Likewise, think of that daily slog to the station, even when it's raining, as a 'power walk' and even 'de-cluttering' has a more upbeat ring than boring old 'housework'.

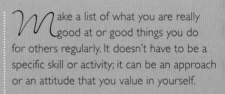

Make a list of what you are really good at or good things you do for others regularly. It doesn't have to be a specific skill or activity; it can be an approach or an attitude that you value in yourself.

Do you always stay cool and collected, even in stressful situations? Are you patient with people? Do you always see the funny side of things? Are you always there for your friends? Focusing on your attributes helps build up confidence while distracting you from those parts of yourself that you think are flawed.

This is the day you are going to move on from anything that is worrying you. Things often don't run as smoothly as we would like, but the secret in these situations is not to dwell on the negatives.

When the going gets tough you need to try to think about how important this or that is in the grand scheme of your life and turn it round to your advantage. For example, so what if you didn't get that dream job? Your would-be employers are the losers, not you, and if your partner leaves you for someone else, perhaps you are better off without him.

Whether you tried out several ideas this month or just one, you might like to reflect on what you chose to try and why, and if it worked for you.

1. How many activities did you try this month?

- 1–3 activities ☐
- 4–10 activities ☐
- 11–20 activities ☐
- 21–30 activities ☐

3. Which activities had a positive effect on your mood this month?

Use the page opposite to make notes about what worked for you and what didn't.

2. How many did you repeat several times in the month?

- 1–3 activities ☐
- 4–10 activities ☐
- 11–20 activities ☐
- 21–30 activities ☐

Notes, jottings and thoughts

Up your earning power

Think of six ways in which you could boost your earning power so that at the end of the month you have more than you need to meet your own requirements. Make sure these ways are things that, once achieved, you will respect and admire yourself for.

For example, is it time to update or re-think your career plan? Do you need to develop new skills or go on a training course? Maybe you need to ask for a pay rise, or if this is out of the question, move to a better-paid job. Make a plan for the future and fast-forward it now.

Allow yourself to make at least one mistake every day without beating yourself up. The reason? It will encourage you to try out things you might otherwise have avoided for fear of messing up and embarrassing yourself.

So, go on, try that hi-tech machine in the gym, hire a tandem with a friend or put yourself forward for karaoke on Friday night at the wine bar.

Diving into a fresh new experience triggers the production of dopamine, which is one of the body's feel-good, confidence-boosting hormones, and how good is that?

215

Banish the S-word

We all say 'sorry' far too often, especially when we are in the midst of negotiating, be it over the price of a car or an annual pay rise. And all it says about you is 'I am not really confident about what I am about to say.'

So next time you find yourself saying 'sorry' just stop and think about it. Are you really sorry? If not, you might need to rephrase fast. It may seem unnatural at first, but make a conscious effort not to apologize all the time. Also try to avoid apologetic body language such as looking down at your feet when asking for something.

Instant confidence

BE ESSENTIAL
Wake up your system with clary sage essential oil. Put a couple of drops into warm water, then inhale deeply before gently splashing water onto your face.

Still not sure how to make your life a more confident experience? Try stepping out of the safe zone and getting some professional advice. Big life changes can take time, but even a one-off session with a life coach can work motivational wonders and help you discover tips and strategies to boost your self-esteem.

Also look out for weekend workshops and see what is available in your area. Many life coaches offer over-the-phone sessions if you don't think you'll feel comfortable with face-to-face meetings.

It takes only one person to change your life — you.
Ruth Casey

Know your worth

Remember you are in your job, your relationship or friendship because the other people want you there.

When you are at work, try not to think that your employers are doing you a favor by giving you a promotion or a pay rise, try to look at it from a different, positive and more confident, perspective.

You are an asset they want to keep and you are only asking for recognition of your worth. The same goes for negotiating with friends, family and your partner. You are an equal in all these relationships and have just as much right as the other person to ask for, and get, what you are worth.

If you want to build up your confidence as a public speaker or are constantly worried about fluffing your lines before making a big speech, try reciting your lines at the same time as doing something else. For example, you could try going over them while exercising, such as bouncing up and down on a Swiss exercise ball (say them to yourself if you are in a public place).

Alternatively, go over your words while peeling the potatoes or doing the washing up. Once you have mastered them and realize you can make your speech despite outside distractions it will become second nature. Nothing will throw you on the day.

OK, so you forgot your mother's birthday, the day of your co-worker's operation or the promise of help that you made to your friend. You feel guilty and start to hate yourself and, before you know it, your self-esteem has taken a BIG nose dive.

Don't go down this negative path to nowhere. Instead, let go of the guilt. Imagine it floating away like a bubble, never to haunt you again. For future reference, make up your mind not to try to be all things to all people and to be more discerning about the promises you make.

Defeat may be a stepping stone or stumbling block according to the way you accept it.

Napoleon Hill

Comparing yourself negatively with others can quickly dent your self-confidence. The trick is not to put people on pedestals. On the exterior people may appear to have it all, but appearances can be deceptive and how can you possibly tell what is really going on inside?

Making negative comparisons about yourself is simply a way of doing yourself down, big time. Instead, take a moment to think about all the great things that are going on in your life, such as your friends and your family; things some people don't have.

Instant confidence

WASH THAT CAR
Give your car a thorough clean, inside and out. Polish the bodywork, wash the windows and clear away all old bits of paper. You'll feel much more confident next time you go for a spin.

Over-apologizing never did anyone any favors, so don't go down that route. It won't make the situation better, nor will it make people like you more. If something goes wrong, say 'sorry' confidently and leave it at that.

The main thing is to make your apology with conviction, so that it sounds as though you really mean it. If you push the point it can actually weaken the apology as well as your own self-esteem, plus the other person's respect for you, too.

It's not how much you earn that makes you financially confident, but how much you manage to save! Ask a friend round and go through your outgoings together. This will make what can be a painful exercise a much more enjoyable task. Set targets, then challenge each other to see who can cut back the most during the coming months. Alternatively make a reciprocal arrangement whereby you help your friend reduce her spending by 25 per cent and she does the same for you.

There can be no new miracles when you are holding on to the old stuff. Pain is a signal to let go, give something up, open up and try something new.

Robert Holden

Confident people are decisive, but what if you are a serial ditherer? For example, supposing you can't decide whether to take another job in PR or retrain as a lawyer? The answer is to try visualizing your two options, to help you see the possible outcomes of the choices you face.

First try to see yourself living with your first decision, then the second. Imagine yourself as a student at college compared with the daily routine of going to an office every day. Really see yourself living with your decision. Looking at your options in this thoughtful way will make it easier for you to decide what to do and then to live with it.

Set yourself a deadline

224

Deadlines are important steps in your confidence journey, helping to keep you focused on your goal. For example, if you want to lose weight by the end of the year, then make January 31 your deadline and work backward to set a series of intermediate goals.

Be curious

225

At a party be curious about other guests so that you appear friendly and chatty. This puts you firmly on the confident side. Why? You are concentrating more on the impression people are making on you rather than the impression you are making on them. This is truly empowering.

Life becomes easier and more enjoyable if you believe that everyone is going to like you. You'll relax more, smile more, breathe more easily, your shoulders will drop and you will appear more friendly and more approachable.

And best of all your self-esteem and confidence will grow. The reason? People will respond in a more positive way toward you, which in turn increases your bonhomie toward them.

Friends and family are bound to annoy you from time to time, but flying off the handle doesn't do anyone any good. The key is to manage your annoyance in an effective and confident way. So rather than shouting and screaming, here's what to do when you feel as though you are about to explode.

State the facts calmly and cooly, say what you feel about the situation and then suggest a solution. For example: 'Sister dear, you've left your plates on the table again. I don't want to spend the afternoon clearing them up, so please, in future, will you clear the table after eating?' Apply these tactics in similar situations and you are much more likely to reach a solution and be able to avoid having a shouting match.

228 Write off resentment

Instant confidence

POSITION IT RIGHT

Before going out to a party or event circle your shoulders, swing your arms backward and forward and get your body into a more confident position.

Carry on resenting someone for something they did and your self-confidence doesn't stand a chance. Instead try to sort it out with them, either in person or, if you find that too difficult, write a letter.

Simply jot down what happened and how it made you feel, then tell the person that you forgive them for what they did.

You don't have to post the letter if you don't want to. Just tear it up and put it in the bin and let go of whatever it was that upset you so, for good.

Try this exercise from life coach Sarah Litvinoff to diminish that thing you are dreading so much:

1. Think of something that you are dreading. Notice how it makes you feel.
2. Form a strong picture of what it looks like in your head, then place that picture in front of you.
3. Now put a thick black frame around the picture, look at it, then shrink it to a smaller and smaller frame.
4. Move the picture and frame to the bottom left-hand corner of the room until it is a tiny black dot.
5. Notice how this feels. Making the fear smaller in your mind's eye reduces its power over you.

There are admirable potentialities in every human being. Believe in your strength and your youth. Learn to repeat endlessly to yourself, 'It all depends on me.'

André Gide

Crystal ball-gazing

To stay on top in the confidence game, fast-forward to your future from time to time. That way you can prepare yourself for the challenges that might lie ahead.

Alternatively, decide to change your direction so you stay on track. It can help to call a 'review-my-future' meeting with co-workers, friends or family.

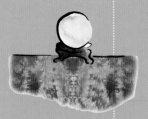

Open face-to-face conversations or those on the phone by introducing yourself by name. Saying 'Hello, I'm so and so' immediately gives you an identity.

This simple act also conveys a clear message to the other person, although you may not be able to see each other, that you are confident of who you are. As a result they will respect you all the more.

Instant confidence

BUY SLINKY
Don't hide in sack-shaped clothes. Forget shapeless sweaters. If you've got it, flaunt it!

If you don't get the job or promotion you wanted, don't let it knock you back. See it as feedback rather than failure and think about what you can learn from it.

The important thing to bear in mind is that it is not you as a person who is being rejected, rather that your skills and style may not be appropriate to the job on offer.

Inaction breeds doubt and fear. Action breeds confidence and courage. If you want to conquer fear, do not sit home and think about it. Go out and get busy.

Dale Carnegie

It is easy to pinpoint what you don't like about work, but you can turn it around and really think about what matters to you during your working day.

It could be getting out of the house, meeting your friends in the office, sharing your knowledge with others or simply problem solving.

Think carefully and write down your answers on paper. Does your work align with your values? It needs to if you are to be fully empowered and confident.

Speak up

Are you terrified of public speaking? The secret is to start small. OK, you may not be able to give the best man's/woman's speech at your girlfriend's wedding, but you can speak up in the Monday morning meeting at work.

The key is to take any opportunity for public speaking that comes up in social or informal gatherings and watch your confidence grow.

When asked to do an office task they feel they are not trained to do, rather than adopting avoidance tactics, the confident person asks for some training.

Alternatively, if they find themselves struggling with a job, they make it their business to find out where they can acquire the necessary skills to help them do it faster and more efficiently.

Next time you find yourself in a similar situation take a leaf out of the confident person's book.

236 Follow up promises

A promised pay rise that never materializes can quickly erode workplace confidence. Remind the boss what was agreed. If the response is positive, good, but if you get a brush-off at least rest confident in the fact that you have followed things through. Confidence grows from taking action.

237 Question your friends

Check out your friends. If you spend time with hopeless underachievers ask yourself why. Do they make you feel better about yourself? Do you feel sorry for them? Go on hanging out with them and you risk becoming like them. It's time to mix with winners and become one yourself.

Sometimes even the prospect of going to a social event such as a party or a wedding can be daunting. But don't for a moment think you are the only person in the world to feel like this. Even the most outwardly self-assured will own up to having butterflies, so what's their secret? It's simple: they hide their nerves, and you can too.

Acting 'as if', as psychologists call it, makes others around you respond positively and as soon as they start to do so your confidence will grow. You could be amazed at how far a bit of acting can take you and the number of people around you who are doing exactly the same thing.

A joyful life is an individual creation that cannot be copied from a recipe.
Mihaly Csikszentmihalyi

Create a confidence jar

Every time someone says something that makes you feel good about how you look or what you are doing, write it down, or make a mental note and jot it down later.

When you get home, put the note in a jar and label it 'Good things about me'. Decorate the container however you like. Keep adding notes every day and go back and read over them whenever you need to give your confidence a boost, or even when you don't feel as though you do.

Don't pretend you know something about something when you don't. For example, if someone asks you for your opinion on the latest political question, the line-up of stars for the Oscars, the crazy prices being asked for most recent Damien Hirst, or who you think is going to win the football, be honest.

If you haven't a clue what the answer might be, admit as much and show a polite interest ('I haven't really been following the Oscars this year, have you got a favorite?') or change the subject quickly ('I prefer tennis to football, what other sport do you follow?'). The secret is not to try to be all things to all people. You will come across as more confident if you talk about what you actually know about and enjoy doing.

Instant confidence

HAVE FUN
Go paintballing or sign up for a sculpture course. OK, it might be messy, but see how your spirits soar.

Think of a time when you were feeling low in self-esteem and someone drew you out of yourself and helped you back on the road to confidence. Remember how they did it, the words they used and the actions they took.

Now go and do the same for someone else. Help someone who seems to be drowning in a sea of self-doubt to recognize their unique, positive qualities and appreciate just how much they have to offer to the world. You too will benefit. Instilling self-belief in another person is a sure-fire way of boosting yours.

Check out your local thrift store and see if they need any volunteers or take your elderly neighbor out for a drive in the country.

Helping the people around you and feeling that you are making a positive difference to their lives means you are being a positive force in the world. This boosts your self-confidence. And the confidence that you have earned is the most long-lasting.

Whether you tried out several ideas this month or just one, you might like to reflect on what you chose to try and why, and if it worked for you.

1. How many activities did you try this month?

* 1–3 activities ☐
* 4–10 activities ☐
* 11–20 activities ☐
* 21–30 activities ☐

2. How many did you repeat several times in the month?

* 1–3 activities ☐
* 4–10 activities ☐
* 11–20 activities ☐
* 21–30 activities ☐

3. Which activities had a positive effect on your mood this month?

Use the page opposite to make notes about what worked for you and what didn't.

Notes, jottings and thoughts

Instant confidence

FOLLOW THROUGH

Here's a tip to help you to stand confidently and walk tall all day long. Try dressing in the same color, from top to toe.

OK, friends and family may think you have really lost it now, but some people believe that talking to yourself can help boost those confidence levels as well as increasing the number of positive thoughts you have through the day.

Make a recording of yourself talking about your great achievements and how successful you have been. Then play it back to yourself in those moments of creeping self-doubt.

If you want things to be different, perhaps the answer is to become different yourself.

Norman Vincent Peale

Have you ever thought of joining a group or club where the members do something you've always wanted to do or know more about? For example, you could try a gardening club, a cooking group, a knitting group, a book club, a chess club, a computer club, a skiing club or a hiking club. There's bound to be something on offer that appeals to you. Look in your local newspaper to get some ideas or check out the Internet.

Joining a club is also a great way to expand your social horizons. You'll meet new people and get to exchange views about new ideas.

245 | Uncross them

PAUSE IT
Feeling panicky before a big event? Try pausing for a quiet moment before you arrive at the door. Then take ten deep breaths: instant confidence guaranteed.

Resist the temptation to cross your arms. If you find yourself doing it, especially when talking to people you don't know very well, uncross them immediately. Crossed arms say 'Keep your distance'.

Instead, use gestures that open up your body. Try sweeping your arms out in an expressive way or using your hands to help emphasize what you mean. This makes you much more inviting and encourages people to communicate with you.

Shake hands when you meet someone for the first time. It may seem like a formal gesture, but it creates an immediate connection and signals the message 'I am in charge and confident.'

Shake hands again when you say goodbye. If the meeting went really well, put your other hand on the person's wrist. This gesture enforces the bond you've already established. Only do it, though, if you really mean it or you risk appearing insincere.

Get around the right people. Associate with positive, goal-oriented people who encourage and inspire you.

Brian Tracy

Focus on others

When you walk into a room, switch your focus from yourself to other people. You may feel low in confidence, but remember, it's very likely that plenty of others feel the same way, too.

Watch people's body language and tone of voice, whether it's relaxed or a little too high. Put them at ease by asking open-ended questions that will get them talking, so that all you have to do is listen. Smiling, showing interest and nodding in agreement will help them to relax. You won't have any time to worry about not feeling confident yourself. The result? You'll appear to be much more on the confident side!

It's a good idea to give your relationship the once-over every now and again.

Questions to ask yourself could include: 'Do we still have fun?', 'Do I want to be with this person for the rest of my life?', 'Is our relationship still growing?', 'Do we communicate well and care for each other's feelings or are we stuck and unable to move forward?' In other words, has your relationship passed its sell-by date or does it need some extra attention from you?

Maybe it's time to sever the ties and start a new adventure. Bad relationships can sap confidence, while good ones are uplifting and exhilarating and can make you feel confident enough to conquer the world.

Instant confidence

HOLD HANDS
Hold someone's hand for a quick boost to your self-esteem. Any hand will do, but you'll get best results if it's your partner's hand!

249 | Be proud

Do not fear going forward slowly; fear only to stand still.

Chinese proverb

Take pride in the good friendships and work projects you have chosen and developed. If someone comments on what a good job you have done or how brilliant a friend you have been, don't do your achievement down.

Rather than brushing it aside with an 'Oh yes haven't I been lucky?' or 'Well, I was in the right place at the right time,' remind yourself that it was you established that project or friendship and went on to nurture it. Give yourself credit where credit is due and sit back and watch your self-esteem grow and flourish.

It could be a good idea to get out there and show yourself to the world. You can spend every evening of the week in front of the TV, but if you do that the only person you can moan to about never meeting anyone is yourself. It's really important to get out there and get yourself noticed.

Find out where singles hang out and be there at the right time and be seen by people who might help you in the dating game. Give it all you've got. Strut your stuff and you will look and feel more attractive. Remember, shrinking violets never get the big catch.

251 Find a confidence buddy

Ask your partner, a friend or a close family member to help you stay motivated while you embark on your confident life makeover.

Invite them to come shopping with you, accompany you to the hairdresser or help choose that new pair of glasses. If you then decide to learn a new language perhaps you could suggest they enrol on the course, too.

Whatever your goal, staying motivated is the key to success. And having someone you can call on to keep your enthusiasm up is a great way to stay on track to becoming a confident new you.

Build your self-esteem and that of others by dishing out compliments whenever you can. Counter that feeling of being too scared to open your mouth or your feelings of overwhelming shyness by reminding yourself of how good even the smallest compliment can make you feel.

If you still find it hard to heap on the praise you could try thinking ahead and practising what you are going to say. That way you won't become tongue-tied or, worse still, come across as being glib or patronizing. Remember, too, that the more compliments you give the more you are likely to receive.

Instant confidence

LET IT GO

Today you are going to let go of any long-held resentments and grudges. A confident life is about learning lessons and moving on.

253

Say it as it is

STIMULATE YOUR MIND

Sprinkle a couple of drops of juniper essential oil on to your handkerchief; it's said to help rid your mind of worries, giving you a more positive and confident outlook.

Invite some people round for lunch. One can be a very good friend who knows you well, while the others should be people who you know and like, but whose presence in a room tends to make you feel like the underdog.

Summon up your courage (you've got your friend there for support) and let these people know how they have made you feel in the past. Then ask them about their fears and insecurities. You may be surprised to learn that deep down they're not rocks of confidence either and have their own vulnerable sides, too.

Get a mentor

254

Find someone who you can talk to, who is willing to listen and who can offer you regular encouragement and support. Moral support is vital to building self-confidence. Just knowing that there is someone out there who is behind you every step of the way, in whatever you are doing, can make all the difference.

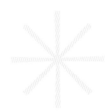

Say goodbye

255

At the end of a party make a point of saying 'thank you' and 'goodbye'. This is an important thing to do as it reinforces your image as someone who knows what they are about. It will help to create a lasting impression of you as a self-assured person in the mind of the host.

It's all too easy to while away precious moments worrying about how you come across to people and what they think of you; a sure route to nowhere in the confidence stakes.

Instead switch your self-indulgent thoughts to other people and think about ways in which you could make their lives happier and more fulfilled.

Putting your thoughts into action will help to build your confidence as people around you start to appreciate what you are doing for them and pat you on the back.

Try to accept people as they are and avoid telling them what to do. OK, they might not always behave quite as you would like them to, but why do you want to control them?

A sure sign of your own confidence is just to let people be, to allow them to think for themselves and make their own decisions.

If you start trying to change someone you may end up spoiling the relationship and resenting each other. The other person is not going to change for you any more than you would want to change for them.

Instant confidence

START POSITIVELY
Start today, and every day, by asking yourself what are the very best things that could happen to you during the next few hours.

Never say never

Words like 'always' and 'never' are not part of the confident person's relationship vocabulary. Avoid phrases like 'You never want to do what I want' or 'I am always in such a muddle' or 'I never seem to be able to get it right.'

Instead try saying 'I know you like to do things your way, but how about giving me the chance to show you how I would do it', 'I may be in a muddle today, but I know I will be able to sort things out tomorrow', 'I may have messed up this time, but, hey, you can't get it right every time.'

The secret is to try again. If you can see relationship glitches as temporary setbacks this will help you to bounce back and stay optimistic and upbeat.

Do you suffer from pre-party self-deprecating thoughts such as 'Why am I bothering to go? No-one will want to talk to me anyway', 'I'll just spend the evening being a wallflower', 'I won't know a single soul and no one will introduce me to anyone?' Stop now.

Instead, remind yourself that parties are the places people go to meet people, old and new, which is why parties are thrown in the first place.

So get thinking about the contribution you can bring to a gathering, as well as the exciting and interesting new people you will meet. Then get out there and give it all you've got.

260

Be prepared

When you are entering a room, you'll immediately feel more comfortable and confident if you've got something ready to say. Someone is bound to ask you what you have been up to, so have a couple of stories up your sleeve.

Other topics of conversation you could draw on are recent books you have read and films or plays you have seen. This means you'll never be at a loss for something to talk about. Also, if the situation demands, you can quickly switch the subject away from you onto a more general topic.

As well as positive, upbeat friendships look out for ones in which you can support and nurture each other's self-confidence. Don't restrict yourself solely to people in your own age group. Forming a strong bond with an older neighbor or a younger co-worker can benefit both of you.

For example, perhaps an older person might be willing to look after your kids for a short time while you go shopping and you can pick up groceries for her. The end result is you both feel good about yourselves and each other.

Many great actors and actresses are shy at heart, but they put on a brave face when they get on stage. However, acting or singing are perfect opportunities to take on a different role to your normal persona which can greatly improve your self-confidence.

So, think about joining your local dramatic society or the choir. Look in the newspaper for details and sign up as soon as you can. If you feel nervous at first you can always ask a friend to come with you to the initial meetings.

Keep nerves to yourself

63

Whatever you do, don't open a conversation by saying how nervous you are. For starters, it can be a real conversation-stopper and also it can seriously affect how people respond to you.

Think about it, if you tell someone how you feel, this is exactly how they will perceive you. Chances are, though, if you don't tell them they will never guess you could be on the verge of a confidence breakdown. Instead steel yourself and present as strong a front as you can possibly muster.

Be an early bird

Unconfident people often turn up at events late. However, this is one of the worst things to do as it means interrupting already established groups of guests. It is far better to be one of the first arrivals. That way you become someone to whom people gravitate; you don't have to make the first move.

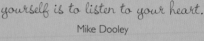

The only way to get what you really want is to know what you really want. And the only way to know what you really want is to know yourself. And the only way to know yourself is to be yourself. And the only way to be yourself is to listen to your heart.

Mike Dooley

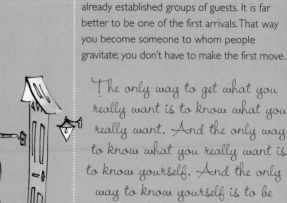

If someone is always putting you down and challenging your self-confidence you need to stop for a minute and consider what lies behind their behavior.

Perhaps they are unsure of themselves and are operating from an unconfident place. This is often the case and once you realize it you can start to relax in the knowledge that in fact you are in the stronger, more confident, position.

266

Listen to them

It could be that you baulk at this one, but friends and family often know you better than you think they do. Indeed, in some situations they may see things more clearly than you do. So don't write off their advice just because they are the ones who are giving it.

Listen to what they are saying and think about it carefully. Remember, you don't have to act on their advice, but there might be something in what they are saying that you can take on board.

Buy a daily newspaper or think about taking out a subscription to a current affairs magazine. Keeping up to date with what is happening in the world gives you the confident 'I know what I'm talking about' air when it comes to initiating conversations or contributing to group discussions with others.

Similarly, make an effort to listen to news programs on the radio or watch them on TV. That way you ensure your knowledge bank is always well stocked.

Step forward

When you make a mistake, don't look back at it for long. Take the reason of the thing into your mind and then look forward. Mistakes are lessons of wisdom. The past cannot be changed. The future is yet in your power.

Hugh White

How often have you been in a situation where everybody hangs back waiting for someone to step forward and take charge? Well hang back no more; it's your turn to be the leader.

If you start to act like a confident person, taking control and organizing people in situations that need sorting, you will start to be seen as a confident person and so your self-esteem will grow.

Make up your mind to learn four new things every day. It could be a friend's phone number, a new address, a funny joke or an interesting quote; anything that grabs your attention.

Alternatively you could do a crossword a day or play a board game with friends or children. The aim is to stave off mind-deadening boredom, the arch enemy of confidence.

EARLY TO RISE

Get up early and go on an adventure before the rest of the world wakes up. It's up to you what you do. Just make sure it's something you enjoy!

Try this easy five-minute massage to raise your spirits and boost your self-esteem:

1. Place your fingers on the center of your forehead, press and hold for five seconds.
2. Move them to your temples, circle several times, press and hold for five seconds.
3. Lightly place two fingers on either side of your nose, press and hold for five seconds, then move down, pressing under your cheekbones and hold for another five seconds.
4. Place your fingers under your ears, circle several times, press, hold for five seconds and repeat the circling move.

o matter how busy or demanding your life may be, make sure you set aside some time for doing things that nurture mind, body and spirit. When was the last time you bought yourself some flowers, treated yourself to your favorite food or did something just for you?

Remind yourself of how important you are and feed your self-esteem. Cook yourself something delicious, lay the table as if you were expecting a special guest and don't forget to light some candles to create the right atmosphere. Put on your favorite strappy dress and heels, sit down and enjoy.

Look at yourself through the eyes of someone who loves you. Ask your partner to sit with you for a few minutes and ask them to run through the things that turned them on to you when you first met. Was it your come-hither look, your laugh or the way you fluttered those lashes?

Asked the right way, you won't need to push them too much to reveal the bits they couldn't, and still can't, resist. But, most of all, it's a sure-fire way to helping you feel really good about yourself, as well as boosting your sexual confidence.

Are you guilty of always asking friends how they think you will feel if you do or don't go to that party, wear that dress or decide to have an affair with the guy you've been eyeing up in the office? If you answer 'yes' you are on a sure path to low self-esteem and it's time to get off it as quickly as you can.

Avoid asking others to tell you how you feel. Start making up your own mind. It may be hard at first, but it will get easier and your self-belief will grow and grow.

Instant confidence

GET OUT THERE
Make yourself heard and seen. Today you are going to spend some time talking to other people about your successes and achievements.

Whether you tried out several ideas this month or just one, you might like to reflect on what you chose to try and why, and if it worked for you.

1. How many activities did you try this month?

* 1–3 activities
* 4–10 activities
* 11–20 activities
* 21–31 activities

2. How many did you repeat several times in the month?

* 1–3 activities
* 4–10 activities
* 11–20 activities
* 21–31 activities

3. Which activities had a positive effect on your mood this month?

Use the page opposite to make notes about what worked for you and what didn't.

Notes, jottings and thoughts

Instant confidence

ACT LIKE A MOVIE STAR

Before entering a room full of strangers pause for a moment and imagine you are your favorite film star. Then decide who you want to talk to and go and do it.

It's good to give yourself the seal of approval at all times and in all places. You are the most important person in your life. Approve of yourself, even when you wish you had done something differently, you have made a mistake or other people are making disapproving noises.

Just try it for a day or two and you'll soon see that it makes it far easier to put things right or to let them go. You'll also discover that showing self-approval tends to make other people approve of you, too, which in turn nurtures self-belief.

I f you wake up in the morning and your morale is low, don't be tempted to stay in bed and brood. Feeling sorry for yourself is the worst thing you can do and is likely to make things worse.

Instead pick up the phone and call your friends and family. They are your support network. It is far better to talk about what is worrying you and, often, sharing a problem helps you to see it in a different light. And, who knows, the day may go on to have some unexpected confidence-filled moments.

If you start to feel that someone has got it in for you, or that they don't appreciate or value you as much as they should, it is time to ask yourself why you feel like this. Confident people are in control of their thoughts and can choose whether to be affected by other people's opinions of them. The important question you need to ask yourself is 'What can I do to change or get out of this situation?'

You may need to confront the person, or if this doesn't work, walk away from the whole situation. Do whatever it takes. You are only a victim if you choose to be.

Standing back and analyzing how you are really spending your days can lead to new beginnings and a more confident future. It also means asking yourself some tough questions.

Are you really doing what you want in your life? Is your job truly satisfying? Are you happy with your friendships and fulfilling your potential?

If what you are doing goes against your inner values, now's the time to start thinking of ways in which you can go about changing things for the better.

Instant confidence

GET A CHARM
Try carrying a lucky charm. Research suggests that those who carry one feel more confident and optimistic about their future than those who don't.

278

Be decisive

Shall I, shan't I? Is it a good idea? Maybe it is or maybe it isn't. These are classic signs of someone who can't make up their own mind. If this sounds like you, maybe it's time to learn to trust your own judgment and become a confident decision-maker. Here's how:

1. Ask yourself what it is you want to achieve, then write it down. Making a positive affirmation of your intentions is an important part of the decision-making process.
2. Now decide what behavior or thoughts you need to change in order to make things happen.
3. Act! Just do it and don't hesitate!

Making a rational choice is satisfying because the clearer you are about the decisions you make the better. But you shouldn't always be ruled by your head. You usually know when something feels wrong, even though logic suggests it's a good idea.

In fact, you'll probably be happier when you follow your instincts. These stem from your deepest self, beyond the influence of family and friends. If you sense that someone or something could make you more confident, although it may seem irrational, trust yourself, go for it and enjoy!

Positive affirmations are key to a happy, confident life. Copy these affirmations and post them where you can read them throughout the day. You'll soon find your half-empty glass is filling up fast!

- There's plenty for everyone, including me.
- I turn every experience into an opportunity.
- I deserve the best and I accept the best now.
- Loving others is easy when I love and accept myself.
- I'm safe; it's only change.
- I'm self-assured and full of confidence.

Not saying anything to your sister or girlfriend after she has borrowed your brand-new shoes and, as if that wasn't enough, scuffed the heels, stands to dent your self-esteem as well as upsetting your relationship. It is far better to let her know exactly what you think rather than bottling things up.

Learning to communicate your feelings to loved ones means that you will be more satisfied with life and also more confident than those who keep silent.

Instant confidence

ADOPT A MOTTO
Make 'Why not?' your daily motto.

282

Love your life

Instant confidence

HANDS DOWN
Avoid touching your face when you are speaking. It makes you look ill at ease and anxious.

When you choose to love your life rather than just living it, you open up your heart and mind and this will result in confident, enthusiastic and highly motivated behavior.

So let your mind wander and make a list of at least 20 things that you love doing. It could be eating your mother's chocolate cake, filling your house with flowers, going for a stroll with your partner in the park or curling up on the sofa with a good book. Whatever is on the list of things you love doing, make up your mind to do at least one of them every day.

If, despite your best efforts, you still can't value yourself as much as you should, here's something to try that might just push up your self-esteem. Sit down quietly and write yourself a list of the seven most important people in your life: your friends, your partner, co-workers, parents and so on.

Then think about your very special relationship with each of them and how important you must be to them, too. If you can't look after yourself for your own sake do it for theirs, or you'll be letting them down as much as yourself. Go on, give it a go and feel your self-love grow.

284

Get a sense of purpose

Your sense of purpose often gets obscured in the daily humdrum of life, but it is important to keep an eye on it, for without it your self-esteem will suffer. A clear sense of purpose gives your life meaning and improves your sense of who you are, as well as boosting your confidence and happiness.

People who know their purpose are more focused and self-assured because they know what's important. So take care not to lose sight of yours. It may be to chase adventure, to be creative, to cherish and nurture your friends and family. Whatever it is, make sure you apply it to every area of your life and watch your inner strength get stronger.

Chart your values

What values matter to you most? Courage, honesty, integrity, having fun or having a sense of humor? Make a list and carry it around with you for the next week. Then look at it occasionally to keep these values in your mind. You cannot have good self-esteem unless you live your life according to your own set of values.

Just don't do it

If you wake up and just don't feel like doing something, rather than beating yourself up about it turn a potentially negative scenario into a positive decision. Consciously decide not to do it for today. Feel the sense of relief and then forget about it.

287

Take five

THINK 'CAN' NOT 'CAN'T'

Today you are going to focus on all the things that you can do rather than those that you can't.

Think of five things that you are good at and then five things you would like to be good at. These will help you to build and strengthen your own parameters for success, rather than constantly looking to others for inspiration and approval.

By building a stronger sense of who you really are and what you are proud of, you will become less concerned about what others think about you. In turn you will feel more confident in your own ability to make decisions.

Make your own treats! Research shows that rewards really can reinforce positive thoughts and behavior. But, sadly, you can't always rely on those around you to give you the acknowledgment you need. The good news is there is a simple answer: create your own reward system.

This is how it works. If your goal is to lose a certain amount of weight in six weeks, promise yourself that if you achieve it you will go and buy yourself a new outfit. It will give you the incentive to keep going and, at the same time, the new outfit will make you feel better about how you look.

Don't ask, don't get

Be confident about asking for help when you need it. There is nothing to be ashamed of and, more often than not, people are more than happy to give it.

There will be a double whammy of benefits. You will be getting what you need to achieve what you want, making you feel good, while the other person will feel good for having been able to help you. It shows that you respect them and have taken their viewpoints into consideration before making a difficult decision.

Maybe it's spiders, birds, flying or heights. Whatever your phobia, it can be incredibly liberating to overcome it. So why not put an action plan in place?

For example, if your greatest fear is flying there are now several organizations that run short courses to help you overcome your terror. Just imagine how great you will feel if you are able to start doing, or face up to, the very thing that you have been so phobic about.

291

Become more self-aware

If you have greater self-awareness you will find that it leads to greater self-confidence. So here's an exercise to help to make you more aware of YOU. Do it for today at every opportunity.

Imagine you are the person sitting opposite you in the train, the newsagent selling you your daily paper or the cashier at the supermarket checkout. Then imagine the impression they are forming of you. Are their thoughts negative or positive? Don't be too judgmental or critical. This is an exercise to raise self-awareness and challenge your self-perception rather than a do-yourself-down session!

Think of the pleasure on friends' and family's faces when you present them with a bunch of flowers. Well, you can make yourself feel that good, too. Don't wait for your partner, friends or children to buy you flowers. Go out to the flower store or market and choose the biggest bouquet of your favorite blooms right now.

If your budget won't stretch to this buy a single stem and either display it in a vase intended just for one flower or enhance it with extra foliage. Put your flowers in a pretty vase somewhere you pass by often or on your desk at work, so you see them regularly. They will lift your spirits, filling you with a confidence in the natural beauty of life. And don't just do it today; give yourself a floral treat at least once a week.

The old saying 'Men don't make passes at girls wearing glasses' couldn't be further from the truth today, with the huge range of fabulous frames on offer, so don't let being a 'speccy four-eyes' dent your self-esteem. Think of it as 'facial decoration' instead and make a feature out of glasses.

Don't settle for the first pair you see. Try on as many frames as you can, until you find the ones that best suit the width and shape of your face. Take advantage of two-for-one offers and kit yourself out with a funky pair for daytime and a more minimal pair for dinner and dates.

Wake up! You are the master of your own thoughts, words and deeds, not your parents, brothers, sisters, partner, co-workers or bosses. Learn to place trust in yourself and make your own decisions both in the office and at home.

The only way you will ever achieve true self-esteem is to obey your own orders and to do what your heart tells you to do, in the way that it suggests is right for you.

Remember, nobody can make you feel, do or think what you don't want to unless you allow them. The choice is all yours and yours alone.

Instant confidence

MASSAGE IT
Massage the muscles at the back of your neck for 60 seconds. This will help to boost energy and confidence levels by improving blood flow to the brain.

295 *Self-belief must be total*

Instant confidence

BE A WINNER
Look in the mirror and
say loud and clear 'I was
born to win.' Repeat
these words until you
really believe them.

A confident person does not countenance failure. They think, act and behave with total self-belief, knowing that they will achieve what they set out to do. Not for one moment do they think they won't get there. They are fully aware that they may have to be flexible and change tactics or strategy, but they also know that is part of the winning game. So play to win, dare to lose and go for it.

Dress up your self-esteem by making sure you always look the best you can. Don't pay too much attention to the sizes of clothes. Clothing companies size their garments differently, so forget the tyranny of size once and for all.

The key to clothes confidence, as all the fashion gurus agree, is to choose garments that flatter your figure. Stop waiting until you lose a little more weight before feeling good about yourself and work with the body you've got now. If you are not sure what suits you there are masses of books and websites out there that can show you how.

297

Be a martyr no more

It's time to rid yourself of obstacles standing in the way of you becoming that super-confident person of your dreams. If you're stuck in a job or a long-term relationship that is going nowhere, it is hard to stay confident if resentment and bitterness are the order of your day. Stop being a martyr and start making changes.

298

Be color-confident

The color of what you wear around your neck can make the difference between a healthy and confident persona and a pale, wan vision of yourself. The reason? The color reflects on to your face, affecting your complexion. For women the right-colored sweater or scarf are key.

ed is the most vivid, vibrant color in the spectrum and also one of the best envoys of confidence. Try it.

Put on a red dress, wear a red hat, try a bright-red lipstick, paint your nails scarlet, buy a bunch of red roses, throw a red cushion on to your favorite chair and watch how people react to you.

While the red frocked date may be signalling that she is game, there is never any doubt who retains the upper hand.
Hannah Betts

How to join a crowd

If you want to make new friends with like-minded people a good place to start is to take up activities and join courses where you know people with similar hobbies and interests will be. Then follow the pointers listed below to get you off to a confident start:

- Look friendly and approachable.
- Have a normal, everyday conversation.
- Don't oversell yourself.
- Build up a rapport with people by letting them know that you are listening to, and enjoying, what they are saying.
- Don't discriminate and don't make snap judgments about people. First impressions are often wrong.

Make a good entrance

Follow body expert Judi James's technique for making a confident entrance and you will be welcomed and accepted straight away:

1. **Pause** before you go in. If you are already in and panicking, make for the loo and shut the door to give yourself a moment to quieten your thoughts.
2. **Posture**. Pull yourself up to your full height, push your shoulders back and down. This action will help to decrease anxiety and relaxes your hands.
3. **Performance**. Pretend you are an actor, a celebrity, a politician or anyone who is mixing socially as part of their job; one that they are good at and do every day. Relax your facial muscles. Now smile.

Share the good news

Shout about your achievements and successes to friends and family. And quieten that little voice inside you that is saying 'I can't tell them because it's just blowing my own trumpet and, anyway, why would they be interested?'

It's time to realize that most people love to hear good-news stories, even though they may not be going through such brilliant times themselves. Positive feelings are just as catching as negative ones and you might just help to lift their spirits as well as your own.

How often have you not bought that revealing dress or low-cut top because you think others will disapprove? It's time to make a conscious decision to dress how you want and to say to yourself that you don't give a toss what other people think. So what if they don't approve? It's your body and it's up to you how you dress.

If you still feel nervous you can build up sartorial confidence gradually. Try throwing dress caution out the window next time you go on holiday or somewhere where you are a relative stranger, out of sight of prying, disapproving eyes. If you fancy wearing a skimpy bikini, for example, just go for it!

Whether you tried out several ideas this month or just one, you might like to reflect on what you chose to try and why, and if it worked for you.

I. How many activities did you try this month?

- I–3 activities ☐
- 4–10 activities ☐
- I I–20 activities ☐
- 21–30 activities ☐

2. How many did you repeat several times in the month?

- I–3 activities ☐
- 4–10 activities ☐
- I I–20 activities ☐
- 21–30 activities ☐

3. Which activities had a positive effect on your mood this month?

Use the page opposite to make notes about what worked for you and what didn't.

314

Notes, jottings and thoughts

Instant confidence

MIX WITH CONFIDENCE

Surround yourself today with confident people and take a leaf out of their book. Watch the approach they take to things; the words they use, their gestures and the stances they take.

Do you fall out of bed in the morning and rifle through the same old pile of work clothes like a robot, forgetting those nice little numbers lurking in your closet? If you answer 'yes' you are definitely in a clothes rut.

Now's the time to give some serious thought to your wardrobe. For starters, hang everything up, but not before taking anything that looks a little tired to the dry cleaners. Then wear something different every single day for a week. Vary the colors as well as the outfits and wait for the compliments to start coming in, because they will!

Never understimate the power of perfume on your mood. It can lift you up or bring you down, in a trice. So ditch all those half-used bottles and start afresh. Your goal is to find a perfume that makes you feel confident.

Go to your local department store and ask for some paper tester strips to try out lots of different scents. Take them home and carry on sniffing. A perfume's true scent can take up to half an hour to develop.

The right scent will be the one that makes you feel on top of the world every time you catch a whiff. When you've found it, go back to the store and before you buy, try it on your wrist to make sure it reacts OK with your body chemistry.

Get floral

Be prepared for moments of low self-esteem with a supply of Bach Flower Remedies. These work by helping to change emotions from negative to positive and there's a potion to suit your every low mood. Try:

- **Cerato** for lack of confidence.
- **Crab apple** for cleansing and self-hatred.
- **Holly** for negative feelings such as envy.
- **Rock rose** for nerves.
- **Wild rose** for lack of motivation.
- **Rescue Remedy** is a good standby for crisis-of-confidence moments such as emotional upsets or public speaking.

Put two drops of your chosen remedy into a glass of water and sip four times a day.

Think about your clothes and the way in which you wear them, then think about a confident person you admire and the way she dresses. Are there any tricks that you could learn from her? Perhaps you could benefit from the help of a personal shopper or a few sessions with an image consultant.

A new image or a change of style can do wonders for self-esteem, so don't be shy about getting a little help from the experts. After all, most celebs have their own personal dressers so why shouldn't you? You're worth it.

You can't go around being what everyone expects you to be, living your life through other people's rules, and be happy and successful.

Dr Wayne W Dyer

Be breath-confident

D o the following breath check before you go out of the front door in the morning:

1. Lick your wrist from as far back on your tongue as possible, then smell it. Alternatively, rub floss between the last two teeth at the back of your mouth, wait a few seconds, then sniff the floss.
2. If your breath is less than sweet, use a breath-freshener or try chewing some parsley or a sprig of fresh mint. If the problem persists see your doctor or dental hygienist. You may need some oral health advice.

Instant confidence

FOR FRESH BREATH
For on-the-spot fresh-breath confidence drink a glass of water with several slices of lemon squeezed into it.

*M*ake-up can really wake up your complexion, helping you to face the day with confidence. But a little bit goes a long way, so take care not to overdo the foundation or you risk ending up looking as though you're wearing a mask.

Start off with a light formula or some tinted moisturizer, coat your lashes with a dash of mascara and enhance your pout with some lippy. And don't get yourself into a state about the odd blemish. Invest in a good concealer and let it work its magic.

Instant confidence

TINT LIPS
Always carry a tinted lip balm with you. Dab it on with your finger to put confident life into your lips and cheeks.

Always check the dress code before you go to formal functions. Turning up in jeans when everyone else is dolled up in little black dresses can seriously damage your self-confidence.

And don't worry about becoming one of the crowd. You can still express your individuality with exciting accessories and jewelry. That way you can rest assured that you are dressed for the occasion rather than being the odd one out.

A good hairstyle that flatters your face shape and individual features is well worth the effort and expense. It will make you feel extra good about yourself as well as saving time on styling in the long run.

If you always go to the same stylist, maybe it's time to try someone new. Word of mouth can help when you are looking for a new hairdresser, so ask among your girlfriends for recommendations.

Make sure the style you choose is easy-maintenance, too. There's nothing worse for self-esteem than leaving the salon looking a million dollars, only to find you can't recreate the look yourself at home.

Instant confidence

BE ENTHUSIASTIC

Today is about taking the positive route. For example, if asked to do something you don't know anything about, instead of being the person who immediately says 'I don't know' become the person who says 'I'll find out'.

312

Belt up

If you are one of the track-suit-bottom-wearing brigade, it's time to switch to pants with a belt. The reason? Elasticated waistbands can lull you into a false sense of security regarding your body image, as there is no reference point for monitoring the size of your waist.

Wearing a belt gives you the chance to watch your waist size on your belt notches. It's also a positive step to getting to know your body better.

Instant confidence

ADDRESS YOURSELF

The confident person has a discussion with themselves about a problem before they ask for advice. Remember, only you will live with the consequences of your actions.

Try to have at least one confidence-building, super-flattering, glamorous outfit in your wardrobe for those days when your normal outfit just doesn't feel quite right. This might be on those 'time of the month' days or when you've had a few too many cookies.

And this outfit doesn't have to be new. In fact, you could be more confident in a classic outfit that you know you always look your best in than a brand-new buy. Just update it with accessories to keep on trend.

The color of that party dress can boost your mood, say the color therapists. Orange is nature's very own antidepressant; it is said to boost both self-confidence and communication skills. And turquoise can be good for anyone who gets tongue-tied in social situations, as it soothes and calms the nerves.

If replacing that little black number with bright orange seems like a step too far, try a darker shade of a color that you wouldn't normally choose, or go for an accessory in a more muted shade. Peach, terracotta or apricot are all good options.

Be yourself

It's OK just to be you. What you see as a possible failing, such as that birthmark on your leg or your frizzy hair, might be seen by others as a charming plus point. So stop thinking yourself down and let be what will be. Try to see your idiosyncrasies as positive attributes and make them work for you.

Put on the heels

Apart from giving you a sexy sashay, adding to your height and making your legs look gorgeously long, there's another good reason to slip on a pair of killer heels now and again. They'll make you feel über-confident. Just make sure they are not so high that you end up tottering.

Whiten those teeth

Make sure your teeth do your winning smile justice. Here's how to keep yours pearly white:

- Brush your teeth twice a day and clean between them at least once a day with floss or an interdental brush.
- Cut down on food and drinks that could cause staining such as tea and coffee, red wine and curry.
- If all else fails and you really want to brighten your smile, ask your dentist about tooth-whitening options.

The right-fitting bra can lift your confidence in more ways than one. Many shops now have a bra-fitting service, so make good use of it. Remember, your shape is constantly changing and sizes vary between different brands and designs.

- A bra cup should cover your entire breast, so that there's nothing spilling over.
- The bra's band should lie flat against your ribcage and fit snugly in a parallel line, without riding up.
- Bra straps should be tight enough, but you should still be able to fit two fingers underneath.

319 Dress up every day

Instant confidence

QUALITY COUNTS
Spend money on good-quality coats, bags and shoes for a confident, quality look.

Think how good dressing up for a special occasion feels. Just doing your hair and putting on your make-up can raise your spirits.

So why reserve 'feeling great' for parties and dates? Every day can be a dress-up day. It may be just another Monday at the office, or a routine morning taking the kids to school, but if you are wearing pretty lingerie, an attractive skirt and top plus heels to die for you'll be proud to be looking your best. And, best of all, if you are feeling good you'll exude mega-confidence.

For an instant confidence-boost go for a manicure. Well-groomed nails make you feel and look instantly glamorous, so make sure your talons are good enough to be on constant show.

Treat yourself to a professional manicure as often as you can afford it because no one puts on the polish quite like the experts.

Color matters, too. Bright red says 'look at me' while more somber shades are quietly sophisticated, especially if your skin is on the olive side. Purple and brown shades work better if your complexion is paler.

Esteem-boosting make-up is enhancing, not overwhelming, so take care you don't step too far out of your comfort zone when it comes to applying make-up. For example, if you are a natural-look girl at heart don't go for bright-red lipstick that could make you feel self-conscious and stick out from the crowd.

Choose eyeshadow and lipstick colors that you know make the best of your features and put your effort into learning how to apply them for maximum impact.

Make dressing for work as easy on yourself as possible. Look out for clothes that don't call for too many trips to the dry cleaners or hours spent over the ironing board. Go for darker colors that don't show stains and classic styles that won't date too fast.

You can always perk up an outfit with colorful scarves and accessories such as a bright belt or bold jewelry. Classic easy-to-care-for clothes in good fabrics will see you through any professional situation.

323 _Dress to fit_

Instant confidence

GO CLASSIC

Always keep one classic outfit in your closet; one that will take you anywhere, anytime. That way you'll have the confidence to accept an invitation at a minute's notice.

Dress confidently, but unless you want to draw attention to yourself don't go so outrageous that you stick out like a sore thumb. It will only make you self-conscious and could stand in the way of you behaving in a confident manner.

So, however devil-may-care your mood, resist the temptation to mix mis-matched colors purely for effect. Unless you are Vivienne Westwood it's safer to dress as one of the crowd rather than the focus of it.

Want to be admired and noticed, but lack the confidence to do anything about it?

Well, an easy way to do it is to change your appearance at regular intervals. For example, if you always tend to wear pants, give those skirts in your closet an airing for a change and the same goes for shoes: switch from flats to heels.

You don't have to do anything outrageous. Making just a few small sartorial changes can make you feel much better about yourself.

325 | Swap those clothes

RISE ABOVE IT
Don't take negative criticism to heart. You can't please everyone all the time, however hard you try.

Can't afford an image consultant? Throw a clothes-swap party instead. Invite your girlfriends round, tell them to bring along their cast-offs, and have a dressing-up session. You probably know what suits you best, but a second opinion can stop you getting too set in your ways.

Be as objective as you can about each other's style without being over-critical. Remember, dressing confidently is all about showing off your best assets while minimizing those you are less proud of.

When it comes to dressing for confidence, comfort is essential. Avoid wearing trousers that are too tight, shoes that pinch or clothes you feel too hot or too cold in. Such items might give your self-esteem a lift when you look in the mirror, but your discomfort will soon show in your face. Your aim should be to feel so comfy that you forget about your clothes.

Book a session with a personal shopper. Their advice is free and will help you find the fashion labels whose designs flatter you and disguise the bits you want to hide.

The more vibrant you make your goal the more easily you'll find it to reach. For example, if you want to get fit, instead of just thinking 'I want to tone and trim my bum,' think 'I want to turn heads as I walk down the street.' That way you'll feel more motivated to get started on turning your dream into a reality.

Even if you are only slightly over your ideal weight, shedding a small amount of body fat can have a noticeable effect on your confidence levels, making you feel much more positive about yourself.

Don't be tempted by faddy diets, though. Following a sensible, healthy eating pattern, combined with regular exercise, is the only way to ensure long-term weight loss.

Be bikini-confident

Follow the tips listed below and stripping off at holiday time won't become a beach ordeal:

- If your torso is long, go for high-cut bottoms with a waistline that is not too high. Low-slung, hipster-style bottoms are more flattering if you want to make your body seem longer.
- Padded and cupped bikinis can give the perfect cleavage, while bandeau styles flatter smaller chests.
- Pattern gives the illusion of a larger chest.
- Dark colors are more forgiving on large behinds, while large prints or stripes are best avoided.
- Choose a bikini one size up from your normal size, as a tight one will exaggerate any lumps and bumps. Try sitting and stretching while trying one on.

Move it!

Keeping fit makes you look and feel as though you are on top of the world and this is why: regular exercise increases levels of endorphins, the body's happiness hormones. It also helps improve your shape so you feel more body-confident.

And, last but not least, pushing yourself to do things you thought you weren't capable of is a great confidence-booster. You go girl!

Instant confidence

POSITION IT RIGHT

Going to a party? Hold that glass of wine just below chest level; this looks confident and comfortable. Hold it any higher and it can look like a barrier to others.

However good your diet, it can be difficult to get the right amount of nutrients needed for a healthy, confident life from the food you eat. If you think your diet could be lacking in any area, it may be worth taking some supplements to make up for any shortfall.

Start off with a good all-round multi-vitamin or try one of the following to perk you up: co-enzyme Q10, vitamin C, selenium or any of the B-vitamins.

Adding spirulina or wheatgerm powder to your morning smoothie can help to give an extra energy boost, which in turn can increase confident actions.

Doing the yoga Warrior Pose is a great way to help center you and boost your confidence.

1. Stand with your feet together and take a long step to the right. Raise your arms and reach out to each side, so that your arms are parallel with the floor, keeping your shoulder blades wide.

2. Turn your right foot 90 degrees to the right and bend your right knee, turning your head to look along your right arm. Turn your left foot inward.

3. Sink into the posture, feeling the firmness in your thighs and how powerfully you are rooted to the floor.

4. Take five deep breaths, repeating 'I am well, I am healthy and I am confident.' Go back to your starting position and repeat on the other side.

Move the moves

If you change one thing today, make it your fitness routine. If you usually walk try climbing, if you play tennis try badminton, if you like to sail try wind-surfing. The more new skills you learn the more your self-belief will grow.

And here's a bonus point: doing something different in the fitness field often sets off a whole new train of totally life-enhancing experiences. Who knows, you might find yourself windsurfing in Tarifa or trekking in the Himalayas.

For a quick confidence-boost choose oat-based cereal bars naturally sweetened with fruit and honey. Oats are brimming with slow-release energy thanks to their soluble fiber: a gummy substance that slows down absorption and digestion, giving you a long-lasting high. They are also rich in B-vitamins, needed by your body to use the energy it gets from food.

Oats are said to boost sexual confidence levels, hence the popular saying about sowing your wild oats.

*W*hether you tried out several ideas this month or just one, you might like to reflect on what you chose to try and why, and if it worked for you.

1. How many activities did you try this month?

- 1–3 activities ☐
- 4–10 activities ☐
- 11–20 activities ☐
- 21–31 activities ☐

3. Which activities had a positive effect on your mood this month?

Use the page opposite to make notes about what worked for you and what didn't.

2. How many did you repeat several times in the month?

- 1–3 activities ☐
- 4–10 activities ☐
- 11–20 activities ☐
- 21–31 activities ☐

Notes, jottings and thoughts

335 | Eat for confidence

Stocking up with mood-boosting foods will help to put you on the fast track to confidence. Make sure to include plenty of the following on your weekly shopping list: turkey, fish, chicken, cottage cheese, avocados, bananas and wheatgerm. These all contain natural tryptophan, a compound that can boost levels of serotonin, the brain chemical that can help keep moods good.

Other shopping staples to drop into the cart include green veg, nuts, pulses, potatoes and magnesium supplements (magnesium is needed by your body to manufacture dopamine, another feel-good hormone).

Throw away the remote control, forget the crossword (it can wait!), give the sofa a wide berth and get yourself down to a local dance class. No excuses!

Go for tango or salsa. Both require you to dress up as little or as much as you dare, which in turn can make you feel sexy and exciting. You'll have so much fun, make new friends, feel amazing and, best of all, be turning the spotlight directly on yourself. And how good is that for building confidence?

Be fishy

> Each human being has the potential to change, to transform their attitude, no matter how difficult the situation.
>
> Dalai Lama

Put oily fish, such as mackerel, salmon or tuna at the top of the weekly shopping list. The reason? They are all rich in omega-3 essential fatty acids, which are vital for the health of every cell in your body, but especially for nerve and brain cells. If these become starved of essential fatty acids you risk mood dips, which can have a knock-on effect on your confidence.

Always go for wild fish if you can, as farmed varieties tend to be grain-fed and can come with low levels of omega-3s. Linseeds are another good source of omega-3s, so sprinkle them into salads or over your breakfast cereal.

Why not go on 'holiday' in your own town? No need to tell anyone; just book a long weekend in the biggest and best local hotel.

Then get into tourist mode. Visit the museums, art galleries, places of worship and any other interesting tourist attractions. Go for walks in the park or explore nearby countryside and familiarize yourself with the local history. Eat out in the restaurants everyone's always talking about and savor the gastronomic experience. Rediscovering your immediate neighborhood can restore and build your confidence in where you live.

Instant confidence

TALK IT UP

Although you may feel down in the dumps, talk about all the great things happening in your life right now. Keeping your conversations upbeat and positive can help to make you feel the same.

339

Exercise your brain

Instant confidence

SEE IT AS A CHALLENGE

Whenever you come face to face with a difficulty call it a 'challenge' rather than a 'problem'. That way you are already thinking confidently and will be able to reach a solution a whole lot faster.

Make a point of doing crosswords, suduko, codewords, Facebook's word challenge; anything that activates your gray matter. Alternatively, learn to play cards, such as bridge, or find a Scrabble partner and do battle with words as often as you can. Stimulating your brain helps it to function better, making you more confident when it comes to dealing with whatever life throws at you.

Relaxed and focused is what you want to aim for to feel confidently good about yourself. Doing the yoga Tree Pose when you get up in the morning will help you to feel just that. What are you waiting for?

1. Stand on one leg. Bring your foot up and place the sole on your inner thigh with your knee out to the side.
2. Then, with your palms together, stretch your arms up to the sky. Hold for a few minutes.

Make the most of yourself, for that is all there is of you.
Ralph Waldo Emerson

Cut out the coffee

We've all felt the rush of energy that comes with a strong cup of coffee, but the high won't last long and you could end up feeling more down in the dumps than you were before.

For a more sustained, long-lasting burst of energy and confidence, ditch the caffeine and switch to herbal teas instead. Try peppermint to revive and invigorate, or ginger if you really want to add some extra punch. Buy tea bags at your local health-food store or try making your own with fresh or dried herbs.

I f you feel your energy levels are on the wane, why not boost them with freshly made juices packed with the life force of plants: vitamins, minerals, enzymes and energizing natural fruit sugars.

Try different mixes such as green apple and watermelon; orange and strawberry; grape, apricot, passion fruit and mango; cucumber, beetroot and tomato; or avocado, carrot and orange. Then, think of your own unusual combinations.

Drink these drinks on their own or blend with bananas, soya milk or yogurt to make a delicious smoothie. As your energy rises so will your confidence.

> Nobody can
> make you feel
> inferior without
> your consent.
>
> Eleanor Roosevelt

A healthy breakfast will kick-start you into action and get you off to a good start to the day. It also reduces the chances of flagging confidence levels as the day goes on. Here are some healthy breakfast ideas for you to try:

- A glass of unsweetened fruit juice. Choose citrus-based varieties that are full of vitamin C.
- A bowl of wholegrain, fiber-rich cereal, such as muesli, with nonfat or low-fat milk topped with a handful of juicy berries.
- A slice of wholewheat or multigrain toast spread with low-fat butter, natural peanut butter or yeast extract.

Try the following exercise and you'll feel taller and more confident.

1. Stand with your back against a wall, with your heels, bottom, upper back and head also touching it.
2. Now gently push your lower back against the wall and bring your forearms together in front of your chest (with elbows touching and palms facing you).
3. Slowly stretch up and try to touch the wall above your head.
4. Repeat 15 to 20 times every day.

Instant confidence

HAVE A GOOD DAY
For an instant uplift change your computer log-in from your name to 'Have a good day.'

345

Get personal

Personal trainers are not just for the rich and famous. They need not be costly and can make a huge difference to your body-confidence. Make enquiries at the local gym, then sign up for a few sessions. Either go for a short course to kick-start you into action or, if you are really keen, make it a regular thing.

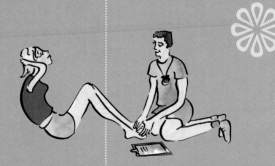

Eat little and often. That's what kids do to fuel action-packed days and they have boundless reserves of confident energy. So try a small snack every few hours to keep your metabolism ticking over as well as supplying your body with glucose. The result? You don't get confidence highs and lows, but rather cruise along on an even keel.

Say 'no' to fast food

347

Would you consider putting the wrong fuel into your car, even in an emergency? No. So why do it to your body? What you eat and drink has a major impact on energy and, therefore, on your confidence levels. So don't grab fast food on the run. Seek out healthy options.

348

Calm it with herbs

Instant confidence

LOOK ON THE SUNNY SIDE

Look for the best in people and situations. This simple approach induces confidence and positivity, both of which can lead to greater levels of self-esteem.

Stress is the biggest confidence-buster of all. But luckily there's a special group of herbs, known as adaptogens, which can help you through those challenging times when life is just too much.

Try a ginseng supplement, which boosts metabolism and helps balance bodily functions, including glucose production.

Siberian ginseng is reputed to be the best choice. Known as the 'king of tonics' it is stimulative and restorative and can help improve stamina, strength, alertness and concentration.

Feeling tired and low can put a real dampener on even the smallest grain of confidence, but, amazingly, a glass of water could be all it takes to build it up again. Most of us don't drink nearly enough, but water is needed for every single mental and physical process, and it's important that you drink plenty of it every day.

Aim to drink at least eight to ten glasses and you'll soon see the difference. If you find plain water boring, zip it up with a slice of orange or lemon, a sliver of ginger or a sprig of fresh mint.

> You can reshape your thinking so that you never have to think in negatives again. You and only you choose your thoughts.
>
> Dr Wayne W Dyer

Stand up

Here's another posture-perfect exercise for you to try, to help improve your all-round confidence:

1. Get into an upright position and allow your head to roll forward a little on the top of your spine, at a point between your ears.
2. Think of your head 'teetering' on top of your spine, rather like the head of a young child.
3. Let your neck muscles soften and relax.
4. Try to do this as often as you can throughout the day, to help ward off neck tension and tiredness.

It's free, you can do it anywhere, at any time, and it's one of the easiest confidence-boosters there is, so put on your walking shoes and find your pace.

According to government guidelines, we should be walking briskly at about 4 mph, for 30 minutes, most days of the week. To translate, that is roughly how fast you would walk if you were late for an appointment.

To achieve maximum feel-good benefits from your walking you should be aiming at a pace that is faster and more purposeful than normal. So stride, don't stroll!

Instant confidence

LIGHTEN UP
Buy some fairy lights and keep them permanently in a glass vase. Turn them on when you come home to brighten up your evening.

C is for confidence

Stay confident and calm by making sure your levels of vitamin C are well topped up. Better known, perhaps, for its immune-boosting powers, this vitamin has also been shown to help reduce the physical and psychological effects of stress.

In one German study two groups were asked to give a public speech. Those taking a mega dose (1,000 mg) of the vitamin had lower levels of the stress hormone cortisol and lower blood pressure than those not taking the supplement. So keep cool by eating more green, leafy vegetables, tomatoes and brightly colored fruits.

Man cannot discover new oceans until he has the courage to lose sight of the shore.

Unknown

A daily dose of the Russian herb rhodiola can help to reduce low self-esteem, according to a study on people suffering from low moods.

Rhodiola is known to improve levels of the neurotransmitter dopamine, the hormone that boosts confidence and motivation. Rumor has it that this herb can influence mood in as little as 30 minutes. Look out for it in your local health-food store.

Instant confidence

GET THE FOCUS RIGHT

Don't much like direct eye contact? Move your focus in a slow triangle from eye to eye to mouth instead. It still seems as though you are looking the person in the eye, but will be less intense for both of you.

354 | Be a fish

Try the Fish Posture, or to give it its yogic name, *Matsayasana*, to help you feel confident and emotionally open. This posture opens your heart and chest area, encouraging you to stand taller, with your shoulders back.

1. Lying on your back, place your hands, palms down, on top of each other, under your bottom.
2. Bend your arms so your elbows are supporting you.
3. Drop your head and shoulders backward so your head falls back and gently touches the floor.
4. Take deep abdominal breaths.

It is only the first step that is difficult.

Marie De Vichy-Chaconne

Lack of self-belief or poor self-image are key reasons why people don't exercise, although they know they should. But there is an answer. A little bit of neuro-linguistic programing (NLP) could help to give you the confidence to embrace the fitness path.

All you have to do is visualize what you will think and feel like after you have achieved your fitness goals. Make your visualizations as inspirational and vivid as you can. What will the new fit you be doing? What will you be thinking? What will you be wearing?

Instant confidence

SPLASH OUT
So your closet is full of black clothes? Try infiltrating it with the odd splash of color for an instant burst of confidence.

It's time to stop choosing things on the menu simply because you want the approval of the person you are with. For example, do you always order a salad when you have lunch with your health-obsessed friend? Is this because you are frightened she might disapprove as you tuck into the huge steak that you really want? If this sounds familiar, then it's time to give yourself a good talking to.

Try telling yourself 'This is silly, I should eat what I want. All I had for breakfast was a yogurt and I am starving now. Who knows, maybe my friend had a big breakfast and is still full.' Or maybe 'If I order a nice steak and fries she will follow my example and order them too.'

The world stands aside to let anyone pass who knows where he is going.
David Starr Jordan

If you want to achieve your confident best, tip-top health is the best prescription for reaching it. So keep a watchful eye on your blood pressure, find out your cholesterol count and watch out for symptoms that could be a sign of something more serious and get them checked out.

Exercise regularly and follow a healthy, balanced diet. You need to be at the top of the wellness stakes to function at your optimum confidence levels.

If you can imagine yourself succeeding in some area, then you can. Nothing you imagine in your mind is impossible.

Dr Wayne W Dyer

Plant some flowers

Build a garden and watch your confidence flower, too. Plants give you something to look after and can bring purpose and meaning to your daily life.

Don't worry if you live in an apartment without a garden; planting up a window box, some pots or a hanging basket can have the same effect.

uy yourself a set of dumbbells and get into strength training. It can help to maintain lean muscle mass, which in turn will help you to develop a confident body image. Dumbbells are the most adaptable multi-purpose weights you can buy and are ideal for working with at home as they are so small.

Use them to shape up your biceps, triceps and shoulders. If you don't know which exercises to do buy a book or fitness magazine. Dumbbells come in loads of different colors so pick your favorite, keep them on show and use them at least every other day.

Instant confidence

JUST DO IT
Do something every day that gives you butterflies...it could be walking into that flashy cocktail bar that's just opened near work or braving the new rowing machine in the gym.

TRY DIFFERENT FOODS

The next time you visit the supermarket buy three items of food that you've never bought before. Try them in new recipes or, better still, invent your own dishes.

Make sure you are seen as a team player at work and in your social life. Look confident and self-assured.

Don't forget, 55 percent of your impact comes through non-verbal communication. Sound enthusiastic, look interested, be keen and totally reliable. Finish tasks and be punctual. Don't let awkward colleagues or friends get to you. Discuss problems calmly, but let them know that you refuse to be treated badly.

Accept that there is no such thing as a totally right or wrong decision, just different ways of looking at things. This will make decision-making a lot easier.

Even if you do make a 'mistake', such as leaving an OK relationship for one that looks as though it has more potential but turns out to be a nightmare, you will learn from the experience. And that will then help you make a better decision next time.

> The most wasted of all days is one without laughter.
> E E Cummings

362 Play the paperclip game

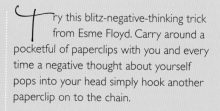

Try this blitz-negative-thinking trick from Esme Floyd. Carry around a pocketful of paperclips with you and every time a negative thought about yourself pops into your head simply hook another paperclip on to the chain.

At the end of the day you might be amazed to discover how long your chain is and just how negative you really are. Once you have identified your negative triggers it's time to turn them into positive ones.

All life is a chance. The person who goes farthest is the one who is willing to do and dare.

Dale Carnegie

Today, try doing everything in the opposite way to usual. For example, tell everyone that they are right instead of automatically telling them they are wrong, eat something that you wouldn't usually dream of touching, wear a leather mini skirt or go out to work in false eyelashes.

Be aware of how acting differently makes you and others feel. To become more confident you have to change your normal routine. You've started to do that today.

Instant confidence

ENJOY YOURSELF!
Write down ten things that lift your spirits, from having a coffee in your local café to freewheeling down a hill on your bike. Aim to do at least two of them every week.

364 | Recognize the good

Instant confidence

SUPPORT YOURSELF

If you get struck by an attack of nerves at a party, try this trick to bring back your confident feelings. Stand with your back against something solid such as a wall or bookcase.

When the going gets a little tough in relationships the confident person concentrates on their partner's good points and what brought them together in the first place rather than the things that are driving them mad at that moment.

So make it your business to support your loved one emotionally through the bad times as well as the good. Remember also that very few relationships thrive on constant togetherness, so respect each other's need for space and time spent alone.

Don't let your worries dent your confidence. Try this simple visualization exercise whenever you feel your self-esteem is taking a nosedive. It can be especially effective at bedtime if you have trouble getting to sleep.

Imagine yourself tying up your worries and anxieties in a helium balloon, then gently letting go of the string and blowing it softly away. Feeling more confident already?

Whether you tried out several ideas this month or just one, you might like to reflect on what you chose to try and why, and if it worked for you.

1. How many activities did you try this month?

- 1–3 activities ☐
- 4–10 activities ☐
- 11–20 activities ☐
- 21–31 activities ☐

3. Which activities had a positive effect on your mood this month?

Use the page opposite to make notes about what worked for you and what didn't.

2. How many did you repeat several times in the month?

- 1–3 activities ☐
- 4–10 activities ☐
- 11–20 activities ☐
- 21–31 activities ☐

378

Notes, jottings and thoughts

Conclusion

Whether you followed the tips in this book day by day or dipped in and out, you have now taken the first steps to creating a confident new you. With luck, you are now enjoying the benefits of making positive choices, surrounding yourself with positive people and seeing your cup as half full rather than half empty. You should be well on your way to determining your own life.

You may not always be able to control situations or what happens to you, but you can control your reactions. That's what confidence does for you; it gives you the power to act as you want to act, to be who you want to be. And if your confidence wavers, all you need do is revisit this book for some ideas on how to give your self-esteem a quick boost.

The road to confidence is not always easy. There will be setbacks, but if you see them as challenges, they can actually help to build you up. Confidence breeds confidence, so convert your new ways of thinking into habits and you'll go far. Finally, don't forget to congratulate yourself on all your achievements.

Notes, jottings and thoughts

Notes, jottings and thoughts

Notes, jottings and thoughts

Notes, jottings and thoughts